Cards on the Table

Leslie Darbon

adapted from a story by
Agatha Christie

A SAMUEL FRENCH ACTING EDITION

SAMUEL
FRENCH
FOUNDED 1830

SAMUELFRENCH.COM
SAMUELFRENCH-LONDON.CO.UK

ISBN 978-0-573-11540-0

www.SamuelFrench.com
www.SamuelFrench.co.uk

FOR PRODUCTION ENQUIRIES

UNITED STATES AND CANADA
Info@SamuelFrench.com
1-866-598-8449

UNITED KINGDOM AND EUROPE
Theatre@SamuelFrench-London.co.uk
020-7255-4302

Each title is subject to availability from Samuel French, depending
upon country of performance. Please be aware that *CARDS ON
THE TABLE* may not be licensed by Samuel French in your territory.
Professional and amateur producers should contact the nearest Samuel
French office or licensing partner to verify availability.

MUSIC USE NOTE

Licensees are solely responsible for obtaining formal written permission from copyright owners to use copyrighted music in the performance of this play and are strongly cautioned to do so. If no such permission is obtained by the licensee, then the licensee must use only original music that the licensee owns and controls. Licensees are solely responsible and liable for all music clearances and shall indemnify the copyright owners of the play(s) and their licensing agent, Samuel French, against any costs, expenses, losses and liabilities arising from the use of music by licensees. Please contact the appropriate music licensing authority in your territory for the rights to any incidental music.

IMPORTANT BILLING AND CREDIT REQUIREMENTS

If you have obtained performance rights to this title, please refer to your licensing agreement for important billing and credit requirements.

CARDS ON THE TABLE was first produced by Peter Saunders at the Vaudeville Theatre in London, on December 9th, 1981. It was directed by Peter Dews and decorated by Anthony Holland. The cast was as follows:

ANNE MEREDITH	Belinda Carroll
MRS LORIMMER	Pauline Jameson
DR ROBERTS	Derek Waring
MAJOR DESPARD	Gary Raymond
SHAITANA	William Eedle
MARY, *Shaitana's maid*	Lynette Edwards
MRS OLIVER	Margaret Courtenay
SUPPERINTENDENT BATTLE	Gordon Jackson
BUTLER	Charles Wallace
SERGEANT O'CONNOR	James Harvey
MISS BURGESS	Patricia Driscoll
RHODA DAWES	Mary Tamm
DORIS, *Mrs Lorrimer's maid*	Jeanne Mockford
STEPHENS	Henry Knowles

CHARACTERS

ANNE MEREDITH

MRS LORIMMER

DR ROBERTS

MAJOR DESPARD

SHAITANA

MARY

MRS OLIVER

SUPPERINTENDENT BATTLE

BUTLER

SERGEANT O'CONNOR

MISS BURGESS

RHODA DAWES

DORIS

STEPHENS

SETTING

ACT ONE

Scene I: Shaitana's drawing-room. A summer evening.
Scene II: The same. Three hours later.
Scene III: The same. One hour later.
Scene IV: Dr Robert's Surgery. Wendon Lodge. Shaitana's drawing-room.

ACT TWO

Scene I: Mrs Lorrimer's drawing-room. A week later. Mrs Oliver's flat. Mrs Lorrimer's drawing-room. Mrs Oliver's flat. Mrs Lorrimer's drawing-room.
Scene II: The same. The following morning. Wendon Lodge.
Scene III: Mrs Lorrimer's drawing-room. Three hours later.

TIME

1935

PRODUCTION NOTES

This Acting Edition is based on the original production of the play at the Vaudeville Theatre, London. In this production two revolves were used with the sets arranged as follows.

For Act I, Scenes 1, 2 and 3, Shaitana's drawing-room was set on one half of each of the two revolves with Wendon Lodge pre-set on the off-stage half of revolve right and Dr Roberts' surgery on the off-stage half of revolve left. For Act II, the surgery set was struck and Mrs Lorrimer's drawing room was set on half of each revolve with Wendon Lodge again pre-set on the off-stage half of revolve right and Mrs Oliver's flat on the off-stage half of revolve left. In this way, the french windows, which had heavy net curtaining, could be used for both Wendon Lodge and drawing-room sets with the patio forming an exterior backing for the latter.

If it is not possible to use revolves, the sets will have to be arranged to suit the staging facilities.

Although this production used a cast of twelve the Butler has only one appearance to make and only one line and this can be said by Mary. A possible doubling is Mary and Doris. Also Shaitana could easily double as Stephens although the real name of the actor should not appear twice because people might think it was "plot".

Shaitana's name is pronounced "Say-tana".

ACT I

Scene I

(The drawing-room of **MR. SHAITANA***'s London house. An early evening just before dinner in the summer of 1935.)*

(It is an elegantly furnished room with a door upstage center leading to the rest of the house and french windows right. In front of the windows is a card table and opposite is a fireplace with a large, winged armchair set before it. There are two display cases, one next to the door and the other by the upstage french window, which are filled with objets d'art – mainly Georgian snuff boxes. In general, the contents of the room reflect not only taste but great wealth.)

(As the curtain rises four people stand drinking and chatting in two groups around the display cases admiring their contents. At the case upstage left **DR ROBERTS** *is showing* **MRS. LORRIMER** *one of the snuff boxes.* **ROBERTS** *is aged forty. He is a charming, gregarious man with impeccable taste and, of course, the perfect bedside manner. His red carnation is like a full stop.* **MRS. LORRIMER** *is a very graceful, intelligent woman of sixty-three. A genius bridge player, she is very forthright yet always well-mannered and expects to be treated with the same courtesy. At the display case right are* **MAJOR DESPARD** *and* **ANNE MEREDITH**. **DESPARD**, *aged thirty-five, is a dashing adventurer with an eye for the ladies, but he is not without thought. If he makes a move he's considered all the possibilities and the outcome first.* **ANNE MEREDITH** *is a shy, rather timid person of*

twenty-five. She seems almost afraid to put one foot in front of the other, but, be careful – when she's cornered she can bite back rather viciously.)

ROBERTS. Do you know, I had no idea there were so many different types.

MRS. LORRIMER. Oh, snuff boxes were very popular in the eighteenth and nineteenth centuries, Dr. Roberts – rarely was a gentleman seen without one. *(She takes the snuff box from him and moves to the fireplace.)*

(ANNE points to one, her hand going right into the glass case.)

ANNE. Look at that one. Are those real diamonds, d'you think?

DESPARD. Oh, yes. They're real, Miss Meredith. Very high-quality diamonds, I'd say. *(He moves away towards the fireplace.)*

ANNE. *(impressed)* I can't begin to think what it must be worth. *(She leans over the case a little more and her hand goes in closer so that she appears to be touching the snuff box.)*

DESPARD. Let's just say I hope he's well insured.

ROBERTS. I agree. A thief could easily pocket the lot. In fact, the whole collection could be scooped into a large handbag.

(ANNE withdraws her hand sharply. DESPARD looks towards the door, clearly irritated.)

DESPARD. Where has our host got to now?

ROBERTS. *(moving downstage)* Strange fellow, isn't he?

MRS. LORRIMER. He actually fell asleep last time I was here.

DESPARD. His manners certainly leave a lot to be desired, Mrs. Lorrimer. But I have heard that his cook is probably one of the best in London.

ROBERTS. I can confirm that, Major, and, if I was told to steal anything from Mr. Shaitana's, it would be the woman in charge of his kitchen.

MRS. LORRIMER. My goodness, whoever said the way to a man's heart is through his stomach knew a thing or two. What do you think, Miss Meredith?

ANNE. *(slightly taken by surprise)* Oh I haven't given it much thought.

MRS. LORRIMER. *(with a smile)* Well, then – it's something to bear in mind when the right person comes along.

(SHAITANA enters. Aged fifty-five, he is the original, oily Levantine you wouldn't trust to sell you a second-hand car.)

SHAITANA. *(moving to the others)* Forgive me, ladies and gentlemen. I had one or two last minute preparations to attend to. I want everything to be perfect, you see, so that this will be an evening none of you will ever forget.

(pause)

MRS. LORRIMER. *(indicating the collection)* It really is a remarkable collection of snuff boxes, Mr. Shaitana.

SHAITANA. A remarkable collection. Yes, a good phrase, Mrs. Lorrimer. Well chosen.

MRS. LORRIMER. *(holding out the snuff box)* This is most unusual.

SHAITANA. Ah yes, that was crafted by Storr and Cooley, the great American silversmiths. *(He takes the snuff box from her and replaces it in the case upstage left.)*

(ANNE and ROBERTS move to the display case right and DESPARD joins them.)

MRS. LORRIMER. I know. How did it come into your possession?

SHAITANA. I always keep the source of my supply a secret, Mrs. Lorrimer. But I have an idea we both know where that one came from – originally.

MRS. LORRIMER. It's lovely. *(She joins the others.)*

SHAITANA. Lovely.

(MARY, the maid, enters followed by MRS. OLIVER.)

MARY. Mrs. Oliver.

(**MARY** *exits.*)

(**MRS. OLIVER** *is aged fifty. A big, rather magnificent-looking lady with wild uncontrollable hair that she keeps brushing away from her face, she is an eccentric with a passion for apples; the sort of woman who is inclined to put on odd shoes – even different coloured ones.*)

SHAITANA. My dear Mrs. Oliver. I am delighted to see you. The evening would be nothing without you.

MRS. OLIVER. How kind, Mr. Shaitana. But I do so agree with you.

SHAITANA. *(laughing)* You're in good form I see. *(He takes her downstage.)*

MRS. OLIVER. Well, I've just finished a new book and it's such a relief.

SHAITANA. Is it about your famous Finnish detective?

MRS. OLIVER. Sven Hjerson. I almost got him killed off this time. Unfortunately he escaped at the last minute.

SHAITANA. Surely you don't want to kill him off. He's made you famous.

MRS. OLIVER. Do you know, if he were a real person I would devise a way of murdering him that would confound Scotland Yard and astonish the world.

SHAITANA. So, you are capable of committing murder, Mrs. Oliver?

MRS. OLIVER. There isn't a person living who wouldn't commit murder under certain circumstances.

(*A moment.* **SHAITANA** *looks from her to the other guests who are viewing the snuff boxes. He then returns his attention to* **MRS. OLIVER**.)

SHAITANA. *(moving to the drinks table)* Sherry?

MRS. OLIVER. Please. Very dry.

(**SHAITANA** *fetches two sherries from the drinks table and hands one to* **MRS. OLIVER**.)

Thank you.

SHAITANA. *(raising his glass)* May you never get caught.

MRS. OLIVER. And may you never be the victim.

SHAITANA. *(laughing)* I'll drink to that.

(They both drink, but appear to be keeping a wary eye on each other.)

Come along. You must meet the others.

(They cross to the group.)

I'd like to introduce you to a celebrity, Doctor, may I present Mrs. Ariadne Oliver, the famous crime writer.

MRS. OLIVER. How do you do.

ROBERTS. Roberts, David Roberts. It's a great pleasure.

*(Then **SHAITANA** introduces the others.)*

SHAITANA. Mrs. Lorrimer.

MRS. LORRIMER. *(curt, but polite)* How do you do.

SHAITANA. Miss Anne Meredith.

ANNE. I enjoyed *Body in the Study* so much.

MRS. OLIVER. Thank you.

SHAITANA. And Major Despard. Adventurer *extraordinaire*.

DESPARD. *(bowing slightly)* An honour.

ROBERTS. *(moving to **MRS. OLIVER**)* What are you doing at the moment, Mrs. Oliver?

MRS. OLIVER. I'm drinking a very fine sherry.

*(**ANNE MEREDITH** sniggers. **ROBERTS** looks a bit put out.)*

Forgive me, Doctor. Only I've just completed a new novel and I'm a little light-headed. Some of my friends suggest that I'm completely dotty at such times, and *my* family doctor has been threatening to have me certified for years.

*(**ROBERTS** is quick to recognize that the lady has a sense of humour.)*

ROBERTS. *(smiling)* I imagine it's quite a relief when you get to that final page.

MRS. OLIVER. I always send up a little prayer.

ANNE. But, you do like writing, don't you?

MRS. OLIVER. I hate it.

MRS. LORRIMER. *(coolly)* Then why do you do it?

MRS. OLIVER. It's better than working for a living. *(She sits on the low stool.)*

(DESPARD laughs out loud. Throughout this SHAITANA has been watching closely in amused silence.)

ROBERTS. Why is it we always seem to dislike doing what we are good at, and would prefer to be doing something completely different?

MRS. LORRIMER. Oh, I rather thought doctors were dedicated to their profession. You're not going to disillusion me, are you?

ROBERTS. Certainly not. *(He smiles.)* If I told you the truth it wouldn't be good for business.

DESPARD. Well, I can honestly say, I enjoy every minute of my life.

MRS. OLIVER. Which for the most part is spent facing death.

DESPARD. *(smiling)* I *love* it. Not knowing what's waiting for me in the next clearing – the jungle fascinates me.

(a moment)

MRS. OLIVER. Tell me, Miss Meredith. Do you like what you do for a living?

ANNE. *(flustered)* I, er – don't do anything. Not at the moment.

MRS. OLIVER. A rich young lady, eh?

ANNE. *(embarrassed)* No. I'm not. And before you put your next question let me assure you, I'm not looking for a rich husband either.

(SHAITANA laughs. MRS. OLIVER looks from him to ANNE.)

MRS. OLIVER. I didn't mean to be impertinent. But, I'm glad you're not looking for a husband of any sort. You're far too young.

(a moment)

SHAITANA. I'm going to be very rude and drag Mrs. Oliver away from you. You'll have a chance to continue this conversation over dinner. But, right now, I have something very important to ask her.

(With this he takes **MRS. OLIVER***'s arm and leads her away downstage)*

(The group gather round the card table and talk amongst themselves, **ANNE** *and* **MRS. LORRIMER** *sitting in the two chairs.)*

Well?

MRS. OLIVER. Well, What?

SHAITANA. What do you think of my collection?

MRS. OLIVER. I haven't had a chance to look at it yet.

SHAITANA. Not the snuff boxes, Mrs. Oliver. I was referring to my "special" collection.

MRS. OLIVER. *(bemused)* Somewhere along the way, Mr. Shaitana, you've taken a sharp left turn whilst I've gone straight ahead.

SHAITANA. When I invited you to dinner, I offered to show you my "special" collection, did I not?

*(***MRS. OLIVER***. nods.)*

(turning to indicate the four people round the card table) Well, then. Aren't they magnificent specimens?

*(***MRS. OLIVER*** *turns to look at them somewhat bewildered.)*

You see, we have an interest in common, dear lady. Crime. But, we look at this business from different ends of the spectrum. For you – a crime is committed – an investigation follows – a clue leads you on – ultimately there is a conviction. Therefore, the perpetrator of the crime is a failure. Second rate. And I, I collect only the best.

*(***MRS. OLIVER*** *turns to look at the others then returns her attention to* **SHAITANA***. She sits on the low stool)*

SHAITANA. I think you are beginning to understand. *(He sits beside her.)*

MRS. OLIVER. I gather what you're trying to tell me, Mr. Shaitana – in a most roundabout and devious manner – is that the four people over there have all successfully committed a crime.

(a moment)

SHAITANA. Not *a* crime. *The* crime. The *ultimate* crime. Murder.

(pause)

MRS. OLIVER. Oh, come now, Mr. Shaitana. You're joking.

*(During the following **DESPARD** gets the chair from upstage right to the card table and sits right.)*

SHAITANA. They have all committed murder and got away with it. Not a breath of suspicion attaches itself to anyone of them.

MRS. OLIVER. *(after a quick pause)* In that case, How did you find out?

SHAITANA. Because I am a clever man. Cleverer than the police – *(pointedly)* – and the so called experts. *(then)* Admit it, Mrs. Oliver, I have a very amusing hobby. No?

MRS. OLIVER. I'd say a very *frightening* hobby.

SHAITANA. How so?

MRS. OLIVER. Hasn't it struck you, Mr. Shaitana, that murderers have a very nasty habit – murdering people? Especially those who discover their dark secret.

*(**SHAITANA** laughs heartily again.)*

SHAITANA. Tonight, I have nothing to fear. I shall have protection.

MRS. OLIVER. *(flatly)* I'm glad to hear it.

SHAITANA. Although I like living dangerously. I find it rather stimulating.

*(At this moment the door is opened by **MARY**. Superintendent **BATTLE** appears there and looks for the*

host. He is aged about fifty, an intelligent, witty, man's man, determined and very fond of his bowler hat and gold hunter-watch and chain)

(SHAITANA, *whose eyes are everywhere, spots him immediately.)*

(MARY *exits.)*

Ah, good. Superintendent Battle has arrived.

MRS. OLIVER. *The* Superintendent Battle? Of Scotland Yard?

SHAITANA. *(smiling)* The plot thickens. *(He crosses to* **BATTLE**.*)* Superintendent. How good of you to come.

BATTLE. I've heard that dinner parties here are irresistable, Mr. Shaitana, and I have one great weakness in life: eating and drinking.

MRS. OLIVER. That's two, isn't it?

*(***BATTLE** *looks at her askance.)*

SHAITANA. May I introduce Mrs. Ariadne Oliver.

BATTLE. It's a pleasure.

*(***BATTLE** *smiles pleasantly now. He holds out his hand and shakes hers vigorously.)*

SHAITANA. *(going to the drink table)* Sherry?

BATTLE. Please. I think I've read all your books, Mrs. Oliver. In fact, I find them most useful. I'm constantly pinching your ideas.

MRS. OLIVER. You wouldn't like to return the compliment, would you? Let me have access to your files, so I can pinch a few of your ideas?

BATTLE. Sorry, my files are strictly private. Anyway, I was hoping to get away from all that this evening.

SHAITANA. But, surely you find crime fascinating, Superintendent? Especially unsolved crimes.

BATTLE. I don't know anything about those. *(He beams.)* I deal only with the ones I can solve. Makes life much simpler.

(**SHAITANA** *hands* **BATTLE** *a sherry.*)

BATTLE. Thank you.

SHAITANA. Mrs. Oliver?

MRS. OLIVER. Thank you, no.

SHAITANA. But, there are successful criminals, Superintendent. Both men and women. (*He takes* **MRS. OLIVER**'s *glass to the drinks table.*)

BATTLE. Women are better criminals – of that I'm sure.

MRS. OLIVER. I beg your pardon.

BATTLE. It's a fact. Keep their heads well, you see. And it's amazing how they'll brazen things out.

SHAITANA. I imagine it would be relatively easy for a policeman to get away with – well, murder, for instance.

BATTLE. (*after a brief pause*) First person I'd suspect.

MRS. OLIVER. (*giggling*) Me, too.

SHAITANA. You both seem to find this rather amusing. But surely *murder* is anything but? I mean, it wouldn't be funny if you suddenly discovered that Mrs. Oliver had committed murder.

MRS. OLIVER. Indeed not.

SHAITANA. But, surely – you commit murder all the time?

MRS. OLIVER. Only in my books.

SHAITANA. (*with a lovely evil grin*) You didn't think I was serious – surely Mrs. Oliver? However, I am being very rude. I really mustn't keep the superintendent from my other guests any longer.

(**SHAITANA** *and* **BATTLE** *move to the others. They exchange greetings, how-do-you-do's etc.*)

Mrs. Lorrimer. May I introduce Superintendent Battle.

MRS. LORRIMER. How do you do.

SHAITANA. Miss Meredith. Dr. Roberts. And Major Despard. (*then*) Mrs. Oliver and I have been discussing murder with the superintendent.

MRS. OLIVER. (*joining the group*) Yes. Do any of you recall my book "Murder on the Menu?"

BATTLE. I do. Very well.

MRS. OLIVER. Well, in case you haven't had the good fortune to read it, Mr. Shaitana, the host poisoned one of the guests.

(The **BUTLER** *enters.)*

BUTLER. Dinner is served. *(He picks up the sherry tray from the drinks table and stands by the door.)*

*(***SHAITANA** *laughs, enjoying the moment immensely. He holds out his arm for* **MRS. OLIVER** *to take.)*

SHAITANA. I do hope you haven't lost your appetites. Shall we go in?

*(***SHAITANA** *leads* **MRS. OLIVER** *to the door, followed by* **MRS. LORRIMER, ANNE, DESPARD, ROBERTS** and **BATTLE.**)*

(They place their glasses on the sherry tray as they exit.)

(blackout)

Scene II

(The same. Three hours later.)

(ROBERTS is seated at the upstage end of the card table with DESPARD on his right and MRS. LORRIMER on his left. ANNE sits at the downstage end of the table. They are playing bridge. SHAITANA is in the big armchair left, by the fire, asleep.)

(As the lights come up MRS. OLIVER and BATTLE enter the room together.)

BATTLE. He really has a wonderful collection. I noticed seven first edition Dickens, an original Goldsmith manuscript... The time has flown by. I tell you, Mrs. Oliver, I could have spent hours in that library.

MRS. OLIVER. Superintendent, you've changed the subject again.

(MARY enters with a tray of coffee which she places on the drinks table and then exits.)

BATTLE. *(innocently)* Have I? I would have thought books held a great interest for you... Coffee? *(He pours himself a coffee.)*

MRS. OLIVER. No thank you. *Not* when I'm talking about crime in relation to Scotland Yard.

BATTLE. Look at our host. He's sound asleep.

MRS. OLIVER. Really, Superintendent, I have something very important to say to you.

BATTLE. *(long suffering)* Very well. What *is* your point then?

MRS. OLIVER. I was about to tell you *exactly* what is lacking at the Yard.

BATTLE. A woman, Mrs. Oliver?

MRS. OLIVER. *(frustrated)* How did you know I was going to suggest that? *(She moves to the low stool.)*

BATTLE. *(joining her)* There was a clue on the jacket of your last book. Underneath a very good photograph of yourself the first sentence said something like:

"Mrs. Oliver has strong feelings about women and their roles in society. She's convinced that Scotland Yard would function far better with a woman as its commissioner..." et cetera and so on.

MRS. OLIVER. *(sitting on the low stool)* Ah – I gave myself away – didn't I? *(She digs into her large handbag and comes out with an apple.)* Have a Cox's?

BATTLE. *(in great surprise)* To eat? Now?

MRS. OLIVER. Good for the heart. It's the pectin in them. Clears the blood.

BATTLE. But we've only just had the most magnificent meal. *(He sits in the armchair downstage left.)*

(She's about to bite into it, but, she hovers over the apple.)

MRS. OLIVER. Do you think I ought not to? I mean, if our host saw me he might be upset, do you think?

*(**BATTLE** looks at **SHAITANA**.)*

BATTLE. What do you think?

MRS. OLIVER. *(reluctantly putting the apple in her handbag)* I'll eat it on the way home.

MRS. LORRIMER. One club.

ANNE. No bid.

DESPARD. Three clubs.

ROBERTS. No bid.

MRS. OLIVER. My goodness. Our fellow guests are really caught up in their game, aren't they?

BATTLE. Bridge is like a drug. Let's take a look.

(They get up and cross to the bridge players.)

MRS. LORRIMER. Four clubs.

ANNE. Double.

DESPARD. Four spades.

ROBERTS. Double.

MRS. LORRIMER. No bid.

ANNE. No bid.

DESPARD. No bid.

(They continue their game as **BATTLE** *moves away downstage and* **MRS. OLIVER** *follows him.* **BATTLE** *checks his pocket-watch which is on a heavy gold Albert across his waistcoat.)*

BATTLE. Ought to be going. Heavy day tomorrow.

MRS. OLIVER. I have to see my publisher first thing.

BATTLE. Mrs. Oliver, I've enjoyed your company.

MRS. OLIVER. Thank you.

BATTLE. But, it's been a strange sort of evening, don't you think?

MRS. OLIVER. How do you mean?

BATTLE. Well, everyone seems to be avoiding me to some degree. I mean, not just leaving me out of the conversation. They weren't even looking at me. I might just as well not be here.

MRS. OLIVER. Did Mr. Shaitana say anything to you about – *(indicating)* – the others?

BATTLE. Not a word.

MRS. OLIVER. He said something very strange to me…

BATTLE. Oh…

MRS. OLIVER. Well – I don't think it's worth repeating. I think he just said it for effect. Knowing what I do for a living I think he was trying to create some sort of mysterious atmosphere. *(after a pause)* Why did he invite you, do you think?

BATTLE. Well, I'd like to think it was my personality and scintillating conversation, but since neither was brought to bear on the proceedings I assume I was asked to make up numbers.

MRS. OLIVER. No – I don't think it was that, I don't think it was that at all.

BATTLE. Mrs. Oliver, forgive me, but you're being rather evasive.

MRS. OLIVER. I suppose I am. But I think we should leave it there. And I ought to be going anyway.

BATTLE. I'll go across and jog him up. Tell him we have a hard day ahead.

(He puts the coffee cup on the table downstage left.)

MRS. OLIVER. How can he sleep? With guests?

*(***BATTLE*** *crosses to* ***SHAITANA*** *and stands over him. He coughs rather sedately hoping to wake him up. Nothing happens.)*

BATTLE. Mr. Shaitana. Mr. Shaitana. *(He leans over* ***SHAITANA*** *and taps his shoulder twice. He kneels down in front of* ***SHAITANA***, *feels his pulse at the neck, then lifts his eyelids.)*

*(***BATTLE*** *looks at* ***MRS. OLIVER***. *She has already sense something is wrong.)*

MRS. OLIVER. What is it?

BATTLE. I'm afraid the poor man is dead.

MRS. OLIVER. Are you certain, Superintendent?

BATTLE. Quite certain, Mrs. Oliver.

MRS. OLIVER. It's just that it seems so shocking.

BATTLE. It's even worse than you think. *(He stands.)* Excuse me everyone. I'd like your attention please.

(The others are engrossed in the bridge game and appear not to hear.)

(then, loudly) I'd like your attention. At once.

(His commanding tone gets an immediate reaction. They turn from the game to face him. Clearly ***MRS. LORRIMER*** *is particularly irritated.)*

I'm sorry to have to tell you that our host is dead.

(There is a moment of stunned silence. Then the reaction, almost a "group gasp" of shock, surprise and perhaps disbelief. ***ROBERTS***, *however, is immediately on his feet.)*

ROBERTS. Are you sure, man?

(And without waiting for an answer ***ROBERTS*** *makes to cross to* ***SHAITANA***, *but,* ***BATTLE*** *steps between him and the dead man.)*

BATTLE. I'd rather you didn't touch him, Doctor.

ROBERTS. Come now, how would you know if he's dead? It could be a heart attack. *(He moves to touch* **SHAITANA**.*)*

BATTLE. Don't, Doctor.

ROBERTS. Let me examine him. You wouldn't want to make a mistake.

BATTLE. I haven't made a mistake, Doctor. And nobody's going to touch him until after the divisional surgeon has examined him. Is that clear?

ROBERTS. You're being very officious, Battle. Why bring the divisional surgeon into this? My professional opinion would be quite enough.

BATTLE. I don't need a professional opinion to tell you that Mr. Shaitana was murdered.

(Another moment of stunned silence.)

ANNE. *(standing up; tremulously)* Oh, dear. I think I want to go home.

DESPARD. I'll drive you.

BATTLE. I'm afraid no-one can leave – yet.

ROBERTS. Why on earth not?

BATTLE. I should have thought that was obvious.

MRS. LORRIMER. *(cool as a cucumber)* I imagine you're suggesting we're all suspects. Is that so?

BATTLE. Of course.

ROBERTS. When you say we're all suspects...

MRS. LORRIMER. *(icily)* I was thinking the same, Doctor.

BATTLE. *No-one* has been discounted. *(then)* I'm sorry. We are all under suspicion. We all had the opportunity to murder Shaitana.

(a moment)

MRS. OLIVER. But, only one of us could have done it.

DESPARD. How do you know that, Mrs. Oliver?

*(And, at this moment, **SHAITANA***'s body topples out of
the chair and flops grotesquely in front of them all.)

(ANNE MEREDITH *screams.)*

(blackout)

Scene III

(The same. One hour later.)

*(The lights come up on **BATTLE** and **MRS. OLIVER** alone in the drawing-room.)*

*(**MRS. OLIVER** is seated at the upstage end of the card table and **BATTLE** is standing looking at the "death chair" with a note-pad and pencil in his hand)*

BATTLE. I'm bound to say, Mrs. Oliver – I find it very hard to believe. Do you really think he meant it? Bearing in mind that you yourself were sceptical earlier on. You felt he might have said it to add some mysterious sort of atmosphere to the evening.

MRS. OLIVER. I *agree* that's what I felt, Superintendent. But, surely, it's now obvious I was wrong. The man has been murdered. Since our four bridge-playing friends were all part of Shaitana's "special" collection of murderers who have apparently got away with it –

BATTLE. There's only his word or rather *yours* for that. *(During the following he turns the "death chair" so that it faces the audience and places the small table by the chair's right arm.)*

MRS. OLIVER. – one of them must have murdered Shaitana so that he couldn't give them away. I think we were both invited here to add spice to the evening. The amateur detective and the professional. Whoever murdered Shaitana must have assumed that he was going to tell both of us – and see what we would do about it.

BATTLE. He didn't tell me. *(He picks up the murder weapon – a long, thin, evil-looking stiletto – from the small table and puts it in his pocket.)*

MRS. OLIVER. Well of course he didn't tell you. If he had, you would have to do something about it.

(a moment)

BATTLE. I was simply pointing out to you what will be said. I didn't suggest that I agreed with it. Now, I was about to ask you if you had any theories. Who do you think might have done it? *(His smile breaks the ice.)*

MRS. OLIVER. *(smiling)* Well, instinctively I go for Dr. Roberts. *(She picks up the score-cards and looks through them.)*

BATTLE. A woman's intuition, eh?

MRS. OLIVER. It has rarely let me down. There's just something about that man. Not only that he's a doctor.

BATTLE. You have something against doctors?

MRS. OLIVER. Nothing. Apart from the fact that a doctor would find it very easy to commit murder. He'd have plenty of opportunity and his methods would be varied and endless. Poison. Under the knife. An injection – diseases that is. At this moment, I think it could well be the doctor.

BATTLE. I can't arrest him on suspicion alone. That goes for everyone. But, it has to be one of them.

MRS. OLIVER. And, if what Shaitana said is true, one of them is a murderer twice over now.

BATTLE. There's an old saying – that things go in threes. I've got to work hard to prevent that happening. I'd better get them in here now. *(He moves towards the door.)*

MRS. OLIVER. *(picking up her bag and standing)* D'you want me to leave?

BATTLE. No. I'd like you to stay. I think with you being an outsider, so to speak – it might put them off their guard. *(then quickly)* But, no interruptions, please.

MRS. OLIVER. I know my place, Superintendent. *(She takes the score-cards and puts them in her bag.)*

*(**BATTLE** smiles wryly, then crosses to the door and opens it.)*

BATTLE. Sergeant O'Connor.

(O'CONNOR *steps smartly into the drawing-room, as though he's been forever waiting for the call. He's a bright young man of between twenty-eight and thirty, eager to get on in the force. He's also a bit of a thespian.*)

O'CONNOR. Sir.

BATTLE. Ask Dr. Roberts to come in, please.

O'CONNOR. Sir.

(O'CONNOR *exits.*)

(BATTLE *crosses to the card table but doesn't sit.*)

MRS. OLIVER. *(going and sitting in the "death chair.")* I would have left him to last. In one of my books, I mean. Well, you always leave the real murderer till last otherwise there's no point in writing the rest.

BATTLE. *(smiling)* Life – is a little bit different, I fear.

MRS. OLIVER. Yes. Badly constructed, one might say.

(O'CONNOR *shows in* ROBERTS *and then exits.*)

(ROBERTS' *manner is brisk and cheery, trying to be a bit too confident.*)

ROBERTS. I say, Battle…

BATTLE. *Superintendent* please, *Doctor.*

(*Having been suitably put down,* ROBERTS *resumes his cross a little more respectfully.*)

ROBERTS. Oh, yes. I'm, er – sorry. It's official now, isn't it? I was only about to say though that it's a hell of a business. If you'll pardon the expression, Mrs. Oliver. Professionally speaking I could hardly believe it.

To kill a fellow when there are other people only yards away is incredible. I, er… well – I wouldn't have liked to do it. *(Then)* Trouble is – what can I say? To assure you I *didn't* do it, that is.

(*There is an awkward moment.*)

BATTLE. *(indicating the upstage card-table chair)* Sit down, Doctor.

(Hesitantly, **ROBERTS** *sits down. There is a slight pause before* **BATTLE** *sits opposite him)*

Motive, Doctor. Motive. That's how you can start to convince me of your innocence. *(He starts making notes.)*

ROBERTS. *(a too obvious heavy sigh)* Ah. Well, now. That's all clear. I had no reason at all for doing away with the poor man. I didn't even know him very well. Of course, I realize you'll investigate my relationship with him. But, you won't find anything.

BATTLE. *(flatly)* I see. Then, I wonder if you can help me? Do you know anything about the other three?

ROBERTS. *(warily)* Well…

BATTLE. This is a *murder* case, Doctor. I'd rather you didn't have any schoolboy sense-of-honour attitude about it. It's unlikely to help matters, is it?

ROBERTS. *(reluctantly)* I'm afraid I don't know any of them terribly well. I met Despard and Miss Meredith for the first time this evening. I had heard of Despard – well his reputation, that is…

BATTLE. And, what might that be?

ROBERTS. As an adventurer. Travelled throughout Africa. A crackshot. Fearless. It's all in his book.

BATTLE. Were you aware that he and Mr. Shaitana were acquainted?

ROBERTS. Why should I be?

BATTLE. Mrs. Lorrimer?

ROBERTS. I – do know her slightly. She's a widow. Quite well off. Intelligent. Well-bred. And a fanatical bridge player. That's how we met. Battle Did Shaitana ever mention her to you?

ROBERTS. No, he's never mentioned her to me.

BATTLE. In that case, it must have been a surprise to find her here this evening.

ROBERTS. I suppose it was.

BATTLE. You've no idea why either of you were invited?

ROBERTS. He's always giving dinner parties, or rather – he was. Naturally, the guests vary. And, if nothing else, he was an excellent host. I noticed you were enjoying the *mousse de foie gras,* Mrs. Oliver.

MRS. OLIVER. I hadn't realized I was being watched, Doctor. But I admit it was excellent.

BATTLE. Now, Doctor. I want you to try to recall how many times you left the bridge table and all you can remember about the movements of the others.

ROBERTS. *(after a slight pause)* It's very difficult, Superintendent.

BATTLE. Well, try. It's not that long ago.

ROBERTS. I think… I got up about three times. I, er – put coal on the fire – well it was dying down. Then… Yes, this is right order – I got a drink for myself. Then, I got a drink for the ladies. No, no – I'm wrong. It isn't the right order. I got a drink for the ladies first.

*(**BATTLE** looks a bit irritated. He half turns to indicate.)*

BATTLE. You have to go right past the chair where Shaitana was found dead to get to the drinks table.

*(**ROBERTS** looks, uneasily, across in the direction.)*

ROBERTS. Yes.

BATTLE. In fact, each time you got up from the bridge table you must have been very close to him.

ROBERTS. *(after a slight pause)* Yes.

BATTLE. Didn't you look at him?

ROBERTS. Yes.

BATTLE. For goodness sake, Doctor. You must have formed an opinion of some sort!

ROBERTS. *(after a slight pause)* I thought he was asleep.

BATTLE. How did that strike you?

ROBERTS. I thought it was rather rude of him. But, then, he was a strange man.

(a moment)

BATTLE. Now will you try to remember when the others left their seats, please?

ROBERTS. That really is more difficult. I remember Despard got up for an ashtray. Can't say exactly when.

BATTLE. And the ladies? Roberts If my memory serves me right, Mrs. Lorrimer got up to poke the fire. And, I could be wrong, but I do believe she spoke to Shaitana.

BATTLE. Miss Meredith?

ROBERTS. When we were partnering she came to look at my hand. Then I believe she walked round the room. Stretching her legs, I suppose. But, I wasn't really paying her that much attention. The only person likely to have seen exactly what was going on was the one who was dummy at the time.

BATTLE. I see. Would you say then that the one who was dummy was the murderer?

ROBERTS. *(after a slight pause)* It's possible. Even probable. But, whoever did it was taking an enormous risk. Anyone of us could have looked up. the precise moment it happened.

*(***BATTLE*** produces the murder weapon from his pocket. He hands it to ***ROBERTS***.)*

BATTLE. The murder weapon, Doctor. You're right. Whoever used it, took n enormous risk.

ROBERTS. Absolutely made for murder this little beauty. Like going through butter.

MRS. OLIVER. Almost as easily as a surgical knife.

ROBERTS. Yes, I agree. *(then)* By the way – it has been checked for fingerprints, has it?

BATTLE. It was as clean as a whistle.

ROBERTS. Murderer brought it with him, did he – or she?

BATTLE. It was already here. Within everyone's sight – *(He takes back the stiletto and pockets it.)* – and reach. *(then)* Well, I won't detain you any longer, Doctor.

*(***ROBERTS*** stands up and is about to make his exit.)*

MRS. OLIVER. I'd like to ask you a question, Dr. Roberts.

BATTLE. Mrs. Oliver, I thought I'd made it absolutely clear…

MRS. OLIVER. Please, Superintendent.

BATTLE. You don't have to answer.

ROBERTS. *(after a slight pause)* Why not? I have nothing to fear. And since Mrs. Oliver has a reputation as an amateur detective – fire away.

MRS. OLIVER. How many rubbers did you play?

(**ROBERTS** *is clearly surprised. This isn't the sort of question he expected.*)

ROBERTS. Three. *(then)* We'd got to game all in the fourth when you – or rather the superintendent – discovered – that Shaitana was dead.

MRS. OLIVER. Who played with whom?

ROBERTS. First rubber. Despard and me against the ladies. They beat us, God bless 'em. Complete walk over. We never held a card. Second rubber. Miss Meredith and I partnered. Third – I teamed up with Mrs. Lorrimer. Fourth. I was back again with Miss Meredith.

MRS. OLIVER. And who won?

ROBERTS. *(smiling)* Well, Mrs. Lorrimer won every rubber, so whoever partnered her won as well. That was Miss Meredith in the first rubber, Major Despard in the second and me in the third. I was a bit up, so Miss Meredith and Despard must have been down.

MRS. OLIVER. And what's your opinion of the others… ?

ROBERTS. Oh, really.

MRS. OLIVER. As bridge players, I mean.

ROBERTS. Well, now. Mrs. Lorrimer – she's the tops. First class. Major Despard is rather good too. Miss Meredith. I suppose you'd describe her as a safe player. Takes no chances.

MRS. OLIVER. And you?

(*A smile on* **ROBERT**'*s face turns into a broad grin.*)

ROBERTS. I always overcall my hand. I find it pays to take risks – big risks.

MRS. OLIVER. Thank you, Doctor.

(He hardly realizes it's all over.)

ROBERTS. Oh. Goodnight then.

BATTLE. Goodnight.

*(**ROBERTS** moves to the door.)*

Would you ask my sergeant to send Mrs. Lorrimer in, please Doctor?

ROBERTS. Certainly.

*(**ROBERTS** exits.)*

MRS. OLIVER. Well? Is it him – or isn't it?

BATTLE. I haven't the slightest idea.

*(But, before she can get on her high horse, **O'CONNOR** shows in **MRS. LORRIMER**.)*

(standing up immediately) I'm sorry to have kept you waiting, Mrs. Lorrimer. *(indicating)* Please sit down.

*(**O'CONNOR** exits)*

MRS. LORRIMER. *(crossing to the card table and sitting in the upstage chair.)*
Thank you.

BATTLE. *(friendly)* Tell me, Mrs. Lorrimer. How long did you know Mr. Shaitana?

MRS. LORRIMER. *(after a slight pause)* I've been in his company on several occasions. But, you could count them on one hand.

BATTLE. I understand. Where did you meet him?

MRS. LORRIMER. In Egypt, The Winter Palace Hotel in Luxor.

BATTLE. *(after a slight pause)* What did you think of him?

MRS. LORRIMER. *(smiling)* I thought him a – *poseur.* Rather theatrical. I found him amusing in one way – and stupid in another. But, he gathered interesting people around him. I feel sure that was the reason for his social success.

BATTLE. Yes. *(Quickly)* D'you know anything about the people here this evening? The ones you played bridge with?

MRS. LORRIMER. I'm afraid not. Major Despard and Miss Meredith I met for the first time this evening. Dr. Roberts I know only slightly. He's a very popular doctor, I understand.

BATTLE. I'd like to know what your movements were, how often you got up from the bridge table, what the others were up to – that sort of thing.

MRS. LORRIMER. I went across to the fire when I was dummy. Mr. Shaitana was definitely alive then – if that's what interests you. I even spoke to him, said it was nice to see a fire. He replied that he hated radiators.

BATTLE. What time was it?

MRS. LORRIMER. Let me see. I don't know exactly – but, we'd been playing about an hour.

BATTLE. Fine. What about the others? They must have got up.

MRS. LORRIMER. *(after a moment)* What did Dr. Roberts tell you about our movements?

BATTLE. You're very perceptive.

MRS. LORRIMER. Not at all, Superintendent, I just think things out. And, frankly, I don't recall what the others were up to. I was intent on playing bridge.

BATTLE. Dr. Roberts said he got you a drink.

MRS. LORRIMER. I'm sure he did. If you say so.

(There is a longish moment during which **BATTLE** *realizes that he is dealing with an intelligent woman and that he is not going to get very far this session.)*

(However, **BATTLE** *now produces the murder weapon from his pocket.* **MRS. LORRIMER**'s *eyes flash down to it.)*

BATTLE. Have you ever seen this before?

MRS. LORRIMER. *(after a slight pause)* I assume it's the murder weapon.

BATTLE. Would you mind answering my question?

MRS. LORRIMER. I may be a suspect – and this may be a murder case, Superintendent, but, there are such things as manners. And they maketh man. You'd do well to remember that.

BATTLE. *(after a slight pause)* I'm sorry, Mrs. Lorrimer. I didn't intend to be rude. Now, please. Have you seen this knife before?

MRS. LORRIMER. Never.

BATTLE. *(indicating the small table by the "death chair")* It was lying on that table next to Mr. Shaitana's chair all evening.

MRS. LORRIMER. Not all evening surely, Superintendent.

BATTLE. Mrs. Lorrimer – please.

MRS. LORRIMER. I didn't notice it. Did you?

*(**BATTLE** is a little thrown.)*

BATTLE. As a matter of fact, no.

MRS. LORRIMER. Then how do you know it was lying there all evening?

BATTLE. The maid assured me it was there when she put out the ashtrays. However, the point is, Mrs. Lorrimer, a child could have killed Shaitana with this.

MRS. LORRIMER. I understand the implication behind your remark, Superintendent. But, I didn't kill Shaitana. I had no reason to.

(a moment)

*(**BATTLE** gathers himself. **MRS. LORRIMER** is a formidable opponent and he knows it.)*

BATTLE. In that case, may I ask you if you have any views concerning the other three people?

MRS. LORRIMER. In what respect?

BATTLE. If you didn't do it, Mrs. Lorrimer, one of them must have done it.

(a moment)

MRS. LORRIMER. *(angrily)* I have no views at all concerning the others. And I consider your question most improper.

BATTLE. Do I have to remind you – this is a *murder* case?

MRS. LORRIMER. The fact remains.

BATTLE. That will be all, Mrs. Lorrimer – for the time being, that is.

(He puts the stiletto up his sleeve.)

*(**MRS. LORRIMER** is quick to note the last remark but says nothing. She gets up to leave.)*

MRS. OLIVER. *(getting the score-cards from her bag; tentatively)* I wonder if I might trouble you, Mrs. Lorrimer.

*(**MRS. LORRIMER**, clearly surprised, turns to stare at **MRS. OLIVER**.)*

It's just that your score-cards are of some interest to me, and I was wondering which was which. *(She offers the score-cards to **MRS. LORRIMER**, displaying a gorgeous smile.)*

*(**MRS. LORRIMER** takes the score-cards and looks at them.)*

MRS. LORRIMER. *(handing them back)* This is mine. This is Major Despard's – he cancels as he goes. This is Miss Meredith's, the third rubber.

MRS. OLIVER. So, the last one is Dr. Roberts?

MRS. LORRIMER. Of course.

MRS. OLIVER. Thank you.

MRS. LORRIMER. Goodnight, Mrs. Oliver.

*(**MRS. OLIVER** doesn't reply, so **MRS. LORRIMER** crosses to the door and opens it.)*

MRS. OLIVER. I'm very obliged.

*(**MRS. LORRIMER** exits.)*

BATTLE. Well, now! I can see I'm going to have trouble with her.

MRS. OLIVER. She's one of the old school. Handle with care, is my advice.

BATTLE. Thank you. Now, tell me – what is all this obsession with bridge and the score-cards about?

MRS. OLIVER. Ah. It's the writer in me coming out, Superintendent. These score-cards give me a clue to each person's character. And, I believe that by digging under the skin we'll solve this murder.

BATTLE. *(smiling)* I thought you'd already done that.

*(A slight pause. **MRS. OLIVER** takes her bag and the score-cards and goes to the card table.)*

MRS. OLIVER. *(sitting in the upstage chair)* Perhaps – although I'm not so sure now. *(She holds up the score-cards.)* And, in the end, these will help prove it. Take the first rubber. *(She refers to one of the cards)* Tame business. Soon over. Small, neat figures. Careful addition and subtraction. A timid player. Clearly Miss Meredith's. *(She holds up another card.)* This is most interesting. Although not so easy to follow because it's done by the cancellation method. Someone who likes to know at all times where he stands – Major Despard. *(She takes another card.)* Mrs. Lorrimer's. The one she played partnering the doctor. Overcalling on his part – and down they go. But, if the doctor's overcalling induces the others to bid rashly – then he and his partner double up. The handwriting indicates a person of grace and firmness. A resolute person who once set on a course of action will carry it through... no matter what.

BATTLE. Very revealing. In my opinion it well and truly sums the lady up. *(He goes to the door and opens it.)* Sergeant.

*(**O'CONNOR** enters.)*

O'CONNOR. Sir.

BATTLE. Send Miss Meredith in, please.

(**O'CONNOR** *exits.*)

(*Returning to* **MRS. OLIVER**) I'm trying to be very fair. Do I suspect Mrs. Lorrimer simply because of our little contretemps?

MRS. OLIVER. I have to admit, she's got me guessing. If she set her mind on killing him – nothing would stop her.

(*At this moment* **O'CONNOR** *opens the door and* **ANNE MEREDITH** *enters cautiously.*)

BATTLE. (*turning to her*) Ah, Miss Meredith. Come and sit down, please.

(**O'CONNOR** *exits, closing the door behind him.*)

ANNE. It really is awful. Dreadful. To think that someone – one of us… (*She's so nervous she's unable to continue.*)

(**BATTLE** *goes to her and leads her to the "death chair."*)

BATTLE. Just take it easy. I only want to ask you a few questions.

(**ANNE** *sits.*)

How long have you known Mr. Shaitana?

ANNE. About six months… I think. We met in Switzerland. At the winter sports. (*quickly*) I was in a group of course. I wasn't on my own.

BATTLE. Did you see a lot of him. During – and after?

ANNE. Well, yes. I suppose I did rather. Parties. That sort of thing.

BATTLE. So you liked him?

ANNE. Well…

BATTLE. You went out with him – to his parties.

ANNE. Well… they were fun. Lots of different people. Nice people – mainly.

BATTLE. About this evening. Did you leave your seat at the bridge table at all?

ANNE. No.

(*Unfortunately,* **MRS. OLIVER** *has a slight reaction to this. It's minimal, but* **ANNE** *spots it.*)

No. I'm wrong. Yes, I did. I mean, just for a moment. Perhaps longer. I went to look at the doctor's hand.

BATTLE. But, you stayed by the bridge table.

(Clearly, ANNE is rattled. She doesn't know which way to drop.)

ANNE. Er, well – urn. I think – um. It's difficult to remember everything. I feel so dreadful. I don't know.

BATTLE. Take your time. We're in no hurry.

ANNE. I – I think I may have... walked about... possibly.

BATTLE. May have?

ANNE. No. I did. Yes, I did.

(BATTLE leans over close to her, intimidating her slightly.)

BATTLE. Did you go anywhere near Mr. Shaitana?

(ANNE can only croak.)

(Standing up) Miss Meredith I realize you're very nervous. But, the only way you can help yourself is to tell us the truth.

ANNE. Really and truly – honestly – I can't remember.

BATTLE. *(emphatically)* Are you certain?

(ANNE is petrified.)

I want an answer, Miss Meredith.

ANNE. I – I... I think I may have...

(BATTLE produces the knife from up his sleeve so that it is pointing directly at ANNE's heart. ANNE screams.)

(There is a quick pause then the door opens and O'CONNOR enters.)

BATTLE. *(putting the stiletto on the small table)* It's all right, Sergeant. Miss Meredith had a bit of a shock. She'll be fine.

O'CONNOR. Sorry, sir.

(O'CONNOR exits.)

BATTLE. As far as I can make out at the moment – Shaitana wasn't a blackmailer. *(He pauses, watching for a reaction, but, he doesn't get one.)* But there's no doubt that he was a very peculiar man. Given to collecting all sorts of – strange things.

*(He watches for a further reaction, but **ANNE** remains unmoved.)*

But, then, Miss Meredith – you don't look the sort of girl who has anything to hide. No dark secrets.

ANNE. No, I haven't. Nothing at all.

BATTLE. Then there's no need to worry, is there? Providing you tell the truth.

ANNE. I do. I will.

BATTLE. Good. There, that wasn't so bad, was it?

ANNE. No.

BATTLE. I don't think you did it after all. You can go now.

ANNE. Oh, thank you.

(She exits with great alacrity.)

MRS. OLIVER. You were very hard on her.

BATTLE. She lied. That makes her my number one suspect.

MRS. OLIVER. So, you're an accomplished liar, too.

BATTLE. When it suits my purpose. Hopefully it will put her off guard and keep her that way until I've completed my investigations.

MRS. OLIVER. I have to admit – she's almost made me change my mind.

BATTLE. Again?

MRS. OLIVER. And I've made a discovery about her. *(She holds up the score-card.)* She turns her score-card over and uses the back.

BATTLE. And that's very revealing, is it?

MRS. OLIVER. Very. Either she's used to being poor, or she has a very economical turn of mind. Somehow I favour the former.

BATTLE. And where does that lead you?

MRS. OLIVER. Frankly, I don't know. It's just a feeling. Instinct.

BATTLE. I did notice that she was expensively dressed.

MRS. OLIVER. So did I. It doesn't add up, does it?

(There is a knock on the door and **O'CONNOR** *enters.)*

O'CONNOR. Excuse me, sir. Major Despard says it's getting very late.

BATTLE. He's right. Ask him to come in.

*(***DESPARD,*** who has obviously been waiting directly behind* **O'CONNOR,** *pushes his way past him and into the drawing-room.)*

*(***O'CONNOR** *exits, closing the door behind him.)*

I'm sorry to have kept you waiting, Major.

*(***DESPARD** *moves towards* **BATTLE.** *Then he notices the stiletto which* **BATTLE** *has left on the small table. His hand shoots out and picks it up and holds it in the ready-to-kill position, directly pointing at* **BATTLE'S** *chest. It startles both* **BATTLE** *and* **MRS. OLIVER.** *Clearly, he is a man used to weapons and killing.)*

DESPARD. Sorry. Did I scare you?

BATTLE. Put it down, please Major. It's highly dangerous.

*(***DESPARD** *weighs the stiletto in his hand. Then tantalizingly he turns it over in his hand.)*

DESPARD. Beautiful. Instant death – in the right hands.

(Finally, he replaces it in its original position on the side table. **BATTLE** *looks very relieved.)*

BATTLE. Major Despard, was this evening the first time you'd been invited here?

DESPARD. I came here to a party a couple of weeks ago.

BATTLE. *(gingerly indicating the knife)* Did you see this then?

DESPARD. *(laughing)* Yes. Yes, I did. But I didn't mark it down for future use.

BATTLE. I wasn't suggesting that…

DESPARD. I think you were! (*He sits in the "death chair."*)

BATTLE. Were you aware that Shaitana was a bit of a tormenter? The sort of person who loves to pull the wings off a fly?

DESPARD. Except that it wasn't a fly this evening, Superintendent. It was a wasp.

MRS. OLIVER. May I ask the major a question, Superintendent?

BATTLE. If you must, Mrs. Oliver.

MRS. OLIVER. You don't seem to be at all upset by Shaitana's death, Major. Why?

DESPARD. I've seen death many times. Some deserve it, some don't. But, it all adds up to the same thing. There's nothing anyone can do about it.

MRS. OLIVER. Did he deserve it?

DESPARD. I don't know. (*then*) I'm not sure if he was aware of it, but, Mr. Shaitana led a more dangerous life than I do. Someone was bound to get him sooner or later.

BATTLE. That remark suggests you appear to know more about Shaitana than you're letting on, Major.

DESPARD. I keep my ear to the ground. Shaitana had lots of acquaintances – lots of hangers on – but no friends. And, I tell you this – I disliked him intensely. He made the toe of my boot itch. But, I didn't dislike him enough to murder him.

MRS. OLIVER. But, you wouldn't have had any compunctions about killing him if it was necessary?

DESPARD. (*smiling*) I don't suppose any of us would.

(*a moment*)

BATTLE. It appears, Major, that Shaitana either had – or thought he had – information which implicated each one of you in a serious crime.

(*a moment*)

DESPARD. In that case – I wish I had done it myself.

(*another moment*)

BATTLE. That will be all for now, Major.

(**DESPARD** *gets up and moves towards the door.*)

MRS. OLIVER. Major?

DESPARD. Mrs. Oliver? *(He turns back.)*

MRS. OLIVER. Of the four of you, who would *you* say is the best bridge player?

(a moment)

(**DESPARD**'s *brow creases, he's clearly puzzled.*)

DESPARD. Mrs. Lorrimer. Undoubtedly. Quite brilliant, in fact. Partnering Roberts, she actually made a grand slam, doubled and redoubled when most people would have gone two down. Why?

MRS. OLIVER. I understand you're pretty good yourself.

DESPARD. Well, I'd hardly say so myself, would I?

MRS. OLIVER. Oh?

DESPARD. It'd give too much away. *(then, smiling broadly)* About my character, I mean. *(He makes for the door again.)*

BATTLE. By the way, you're not thinking of leaving for foreign parts in the near future, are you?

DESPARD. I'll keep in touch.

(**DESPARD** *exits.*)

MRS. OLIVER. An intelligent man.

BATTLE. Intelligent men are always dangerous.

(There is a moment between them.)

MRS. OLIVER. Where do you start?

BATTLE. A look into the past, I suppose. See what I can dig up.

MRS. OLIVER. *(hesitantly)* Er – have you any objection to me doing a bit of "amateur detective" work?

BATTLE. *(after a slight pause)* Would it make any difference if I said no?

MRS. OLIVER. *(smiling broadly)* None whatsoever.

BATTLE. I warn you. Be very careful. Someone who's murdered twice will not hesitate to murder again.

MRS. OLIVER. Do you think there will be another murder?

BATTLE. *(after a slight pause)* It's on the cards. *(He takes the score-cards.)* Mrs. Oliver Well, *I* don't intend to be the victim.

(a moment)

BATTLE. I'm sure you don't.

(blackout)

Scene IV

(The Lights come up on **DR. ROBERTS**' *surgery, left.)*

(There is a door extreme left, with a desk, two chairs and a background of shelves filled with books. Either side of the shelves are pictures with the one nearest the door askew.)

(The surgery is empty but we hear the voices of **MISS BURGESS**, *the doctor's secretary, and* **BATTLE** *offstage.)*

MISS BURGESS. *(off)* I really don't know that I can allow this, Superintendent.

BATTLE. *(off)* Oh but, Miss Burgess, please. It will only take a moment. I'm not trying to pillory the doctor. I'm hoping to clear him.

MISS BURGESS. *(off)* Well, I think you'll have to come back when the doctor's here.

(The telephone rings onstage.)

(pff) Excuse me.

BATTLE. *(off)* But it'll be highly inconvenient, Miss Burgess.

MISS BURGESS. *(off)* Excuse me.

(The phone rings for the second time.)

*(***MISS BURGESS** *enters left. Aged thirty-five, she's a touchy sort of lady but susceptible to flattery.)*

(The phone rings once more.)

BATTLE. *(off)* Miss Burgess, I assure you, it'll be highly confidential.

MISS BURGESS. *(answering the phone)* Dr. Roberts' surgery... Mrs. Anderson, you can't expect the doctor to call on you again today – he is very busy... Can you hold on for a minute, I'll look up your card? *(She puts the phone down and crosses to the door, listening for* **BATTLE**. *Then she notices that the picture by the door is askew and straightens it. She crosses back to the phone and sits down.)* Hello. I've got your card in front of me right now... Well, if you'll hold on a moment I'll take a look. *(She puts her glasses on and mimes picking up the medical card.)* Oh, yes,

MRS. ANDERSON. There isn't anything seriously wrong. Only a minor ailment... My advice? Well never mind what I think. Do as the doctor says – keep taking the tablets. Goodbye.

*(**BATTLE** enters.)*

BATTLE. Miss Burgess, please.

MISS BURGESS. Really, Superintendent, I don't know how you can begin to think that the doctor has something to do with it, anyway. He's an honourable man.

BATTLE. I wasn't suggesting otherwise. But, in my line of work you hear a lot of gossip.

(He watches her for a reaction and gets a slight one.)

Rumours. Hints. You know the sort of thing.

*(Her hackles are beginning to rise but during the following we note that **MISS BURGESS** starts to thaw.)*

As far as I'm concerned it's all a lot of nonsense. "Suspicious circumstances concerning a patient's death..." I hear that sort of thing all the time. I can't exactly ignore it, although I'd very much like to. Especially in this case.

MISS BURGESS. It's terrible. Wagging tongues. I know what you mean.

BATTLE. I knew you would.

MISS BURGESS. Someone's got hold of that story about Mrs. Graves, haven't they?

BATTLE. Ah, well.

MISS BURGESS. I knew it. It's disgraceful. Gossiping about situations they know nothing about.

BATTLE. *(sympathetically)* Human nature has a lot to answer for, Miss Burgess.

MISS BURGESS. Lots of old ladies get that particular bee in their bonnet, convinced their doctor is poisoning them. That woman had three different doctors before coming here. Dr. Roberts was delighted when she left to go to Steele. After which she went to Dr. Lee and then Dr. Farmer and then she died.

MISS BURGESS. She was poisoned. *(then)* Silly woman used to bottle her own fruit. Well, you know how dangerous that can be if you're not meticulous.

BATTLE. Botulism.

MISS BURGESS. Entirely her own fault.

BATTLE. Oh, yes, yes. But, forgive me for saying this, Miss Burgess, won't you? I'm afraid it's usually the women patients who start all the trouble.

MISS BURGESS. Sometimes, I'm ashamed of my own sex, Superintendent.

BATTLE. Oh, no – you mustn't say that.

MISS BURGESS. It's true. It's true. How the doctor puts up with some of them – and there was one…

(She stops, not sure of herself. But, **BATTLE** *dives in at the deep end.)*

BATTLE. Er, Mrs. Samuels?

MISS BURGESS. No, Craddock.

BATTLE. Yes, of course. That was two or three years ago.

MISS BURGESS. More like four or five.

BATTLE. Good Lord, how time flies.

MISS BURGESS. A most unwholesome woman. I was glad when she went abroad. Told her poor husband all sorts of wicked things. And that poor man, what a terrible death.

BATTLE. Awful.

MISS BURGESS. Anthrax. An infected shaving brush. Foreign, of course.

BATTLE. Makes you realize, it really is best to buy British.

MISS BURGESS. I sometimes believe he wanted to die. Man mad she was. They'd barely laid the coffin in its grave before she was off. To Egypt. For goodness knows what purpose. Still, it proved to be her undoing. Picked up some native infection. Died from blood poisoning within days.

BATTLE. Some might say she got what she deserved.

MISS BURGESS. Indeed.

BATTLE. You've been very helpful, Miss Burgess. And, from what you say, I don't think it'll be necessary to pursue this matter with the doctor.

MISS BURGESS. *(beaming)* Of course. But if I can be of any more help?

BATTLE. I won't hesitate. *(He starts towards the door.)*

*(**DR. ROBERTS** enters.)*

(A little atmosphere is immediately created.)

Ah. The good doctor himself. I'm just leaving, as a matter of fact.

ROBERTS. *(irritated)* Would you mind telling me why you're here?

BATTLE. Not at all, old chap. Just continuing my enquiries. Must rush.

Meeting back at the Yard. Goodbye for now, Miss Burgess.

*(**BATTLE** exits.)*

ROBERTS. *(worried)* What did he want, Miss Burgess?

MISS BURGESS. I must say, Doctor, he was extremely pleasant.

ROBERTS. *(vehemently)* But what exactly did he ask you? I want to know.

MISS BURGESS. *(a little put out)* Really, Doctor. It was nothing important.

And, in any case, you should know you can rely on my discretion.

ROBERTS. Of course.

MISS BURGESS. Apparently, someone had told him about old Mrs. Graves. I simply put him right.

ROBERTS. Graves? Old Mrs. Graves?

MISS BURGESS. Yes.

ROBERTS. That's funny. That's very funny. *(He bursts into laughter.)*

(The Lights fade down on the surgery.)

*(***ROBERTS*** *and* ***MISS BURGESS*** *exit.)*

(The Lights fade up on Wendon Lodge right.)

(This is simply french windows opening on to a patio, where garden furniture is neatly arranged, with an archway right. Some foliage will help.)

(a moment)

*(***MRS. OLIVER*** *appears through the archway. She is dressed for the country: tweeds, brogues, etc., but she still looks her messy self and carries her large handbag.)*

MRS. OLIVER. Hello, there. Anyone at home? *(She notices the french windows are open.)* Good Lord! Anyone could walk in and strip the place. Still, they do say it's different in the country.

(She moves to a seat and sits down. She opens her bag, dips into it and comes out with an enormous apple. She breathes on it, gives it a quick polish on her sleeve and takes a bite. Clearly, she is enjoying the mouthful.)

*(But, we hear someone approaching, off. ***MRS. OLIVER*** tries to free herself of the mouthful but it's too much to swallow.)*

*(***ANNE MEREDITH*** *and* ***RHODA DAWES*** *come round the side of the cottage. ***RHODA*** is a beautiful, rich girl of twenty-five. A little naive, she is, nevertheless, a charming, steadfast girl, and a good friend.)*

(They are both surprised to see **MRS. OLIVER** *sitting there, trying desperately to dispose of the apple in her mouth.)*

ANNE. Oh! Mrs. Oliver!

*(***MRS. OLIVER** *gets up, still trying to swallow the apple. She's having difficulty, but she does pop the remainder of the apple she is holding in her pocket.)*

RHODA. You didn't say you were expecting company, Anne.

ANNE. I wasn't. *(making introductions)* This is Mrs. Ariadne Oliver. Rhoda Dawes. Rhoda and I live here together.

RHODA. Not *the* Ariadne Oliver – the famous crime writer?

*(***MRS. OLIVER** *manages to swallow the last piece of apple. She takes* **RHODA**'s *hand and shakes it vigorously.)*

MRS. OLIVER. How do you do.

RHODA. How exciting. I'm a great admirer of yours.

ANNE. Shall we sit down? *(She's a little embarrassed by Rhoda's effusiveness.)*

RHODA. *(still excited)* Tea. You must have some tea.

MRS. OLIVER. Thank you, but the tea can wait. I've got a lot to say.

(They all sit down.)

(to **ANNE***)* Now, about this murder. We've got to do something.

ANNE. I don't understand. What can I do?

MRS. OLIVER. Well, now. My instincts tell me it was that doctor. Roberts. A Welsh name, you see. Never trust the Welsh.

ANNE. My name is Meredith.

MRS. OLIVER. Ah, well. That's different. Rugby. Welsh rugby name. Different again.

RHODA. Billy Meredith was a soccer player.

MRS. OLIVER. *(to* **ANNE***)* No relation, was he?

ANNE. No.

MRS. OLIVER. There you are then.

RHODA. But, he played for England.

MRS. OLIVER. Don't know where you are with the Welsh, you see. However, to the point. You don't want people thinking *you* did it. Do you?

ANNE. Why should they think that *I* did it?

MRS. OLIVER. Perhaps *you* could tell me… ?

ANNE. I've not the faintest idea!

MRS. OLIVER. Something in your past perhaps?

ANNE. I've nothing to hide.

MRS. OLIVER. My dear, I've come here to help you. The others can look after themselves. But, you – well pardon me for saying so – but you are rather vulnerable.

RHODA. It was a beastly thing to happen, Mrs. Oliver. And you're right.

Anne is vulnerable. Aren't you, darling?

ANNE. It's very upsetting.

RHODA. *(to* **MRS. OLIVER***)* I can see your point. It's much better to be doing something about it, than just sitting around here waiting.

MRS. OLIVER. Now you're talking! I want you both to help me prove it was Roberts.

ANNE. I don't think it was him.

MRS. OLIVER. You seem very sure of that.

ANNE. Well, he's a doctor. Wouldn't he have used poison or something?

MRS. OLIVER. You saw the knife. Just like a *surgical* instrument. And the autopsy showed that it went right into the centre of the heart.

RHODA. But, *why* do you think he wanted to kill Mr. Shaitana?

MRS. OLIVER. Well, it's only a theory I know, but I think Roberts was in his clutches. So, he murdered Shaitana because he could no longer pay him off.

RHODA. Blackmail.

MRS. OLIVER. What I imagine happened, is that one of the doctor's patients died in rather dubious circumstances. Everyone assumed it was natural causes in the end – but, in fact, it was the doctor's doing. He was simply clever enough to make it look like some unusual disease or other.

Doctors can do that sort of thing, you know. And, I dare say, he's disposed of a lot of patients in that way. Probably to benefit from their wills.

ANNE. I think it's an absurd idea.

RHODA. Anne, really! *(to* **MRS. OLIVER***)* I think it's probably a splendid theory.

*(**MAJOR DESPARD** enters through the archway.)*

DESPARD. Ah, there you are. I do hope you'll pardon the intrusion. I tried the front door. But the bell doesn't seem to be working.

MRS. OLIVER. Major Despard. What a surprise.

DESPARD. Likewise, Mrs. Oliver. Doing a bit of private detecting, eh? Did that man Battle put you up to coming down here?

MRS. OLIVER. *(flustered)* I beg your pardon. No. And I wasn't – investigating or anything. As a matter of fact, I was just going. I was passing and – well… It doesn't matter…

DESPARD. I was just passing, too.

*(**MRS. OLIVER** heads for the archway.)*

RHODA. *(to* **MRS. OLIVER***)* Won't you stay for tea?

MRS. OLIVER. *(composing herself)* No, thank you. I must be getting back.

I'm sure we'll be seeing each other again soon. Do call in on me when you're in town. Both of you, that is.

RHODA. How lovely.

ANNE. *(crossing to* **MRS. OLIVER***)* It was extraordinarily kind of you to call,

MRS. OLIVER. But, frankly, I want to forget all about it from now on.

MRS. OLIVER. The question is, my dear child, will you be allowed to forget about it? I really must be going.

MRS. OLIVER. I'll see you out.

(MRS. OLIVER and ANNE exit through the archway.)

DESPARD. Daunting, isn't she?

RHODA. I think she's charming.

DESPARD. Well, perhaps. I was at the dinner party the other evening.

RHODA. That's where you met Anne.

DESPARD. We sat next to each other.

RHODA. She didn't mention you.

(a moment)

DESPARD. I've parked my car just above the weir – it's very beautiful there.

RHODA. Yes, and very dangerous too.

(ANNE appears through the archway.)

DESPARD. Ah, Miss Meredith. I'd like to explain why I'm here.

ANNE. How did you get my address?

DESPARD. From Superintendent Battle. He called at my rooms earlier. He let your address slip when he explained you were next on his list for a visit. He went off to Paddington and I worked it out that I could just about beat the train down here. *(He turns to look at RHODA.)* You see, I thought you were a young lady all alone in the world.

ANNE. Oh, I'm sorry. This is my friend Rhoda Dawes. We live here together, you see.

(DESPARD holds out his hand and RHODA takes it and holds on. We get the distinct impression that if she isn't yet smitten with him she clearly finds him attractive.)

DESPARD. How do you do.

RHODA. Very well, thank you.

DESPARD. Despard. Major Bruce Despard.

(RHODA is still holding his hand. Then she notices ANNE looking at her and she pulls her hand away fast.)

(to ANNE) It's clear the police believe one of us four playing bridge murdered Shaitana. *(then)* I came down here to suggest you put yourself in the hands of a very good solicitor. *(He takes out a piece of paper.)* I can recommend this man. He's my own solicitor. His offices are in Lincoln's Inn. He's a first class man.

ANNE. *(taking the paper)* Thank you.

DESPARD. With him on your side you need fear no-one.

RHODA. It's awfully good of you. It's been getting Anne down.

DESPARD. Hardly surprising. *(Then)* I'd better be on my way before Battle turns up.

RHODA. I suppose he'll be asking some very awkward questions.

ANNE. I can't think why. I didn't do it.

DESPARD. No, of course not. But, forgive me. If there's anything in your relationship with Shaitana that you'd, well – rather didn't come out – you don't have to answer questions, but if you do it's advisable to have a good solicitor present.

ANNE. *(a little angry)* Superintendent Battle can ask what he likes. I have nothing to hide.

DESPARD. *(stiffly)* Do – please – forgive me. Well. I'd better leave.

RHODA. I'll see you out.

DESPARD. Thank you.

(RHODA exits through the archway.)

(holding out his hand to ANNE) Goodbye.

(They shake hands.)

ANNE. Goodbye. And, thank you.

DESPARD. We're in the same boat, you know – we should be pals. *(He gives a quick smile.)*

(DESPARD exits through the archway.)

(ANNE is very worried and on edge.)

(a moment)

(RHODA returns.)

RHODA. What a charming man. He obviously likes you a lot.

ANNE. Oh, don't be ridiculous!

RHODA. Sorry. It's just that he must think a lot of you – to drive all the way down here. To help you, I mean.

ANNE. *(after a slight pause)* I wonder if that was his real reason? Anyway, he seems to have taken more than a passing interest in you – and you in him.

RHODA. Really, Anne! I shall be glad when this is all over. It seems to have quite changed you.

(BATTLE signals his arrival with a discreet cough and then appears from inside the house at the french windows.)

(The girls turns to face him as he comes out.)

BATTLE. I did rattle the letter-box. Bell doesn't seem to work, you see.

RHODA. We could do with a man about the house.

ANNE. This is Rhoda Dawes, Superintendent.

(BATTLE and RHODA shake hands.)

BATTLE. How do you do.

RHODA. How do you do.

BATTLE. Would you mind if I had a word in private with Miss Meredith, please?

RHODA. *(looking at ANNE)* Well – no, of course not.

BATTLE. *(smiling)* It won't take long.

(RHODA exits through the french windows.)

Sit down, Miss Meredith.

(ANNE sits down. She is feeling very awkward. BATTLE takes out his notebook.)

BATTLE. I understand you worked for a Mrs. Eldon on the Isle of Wight.

(**ANNE** *shoots him a quick surprised look*)

ANNE. How did you know that?

BATTLE. Through my enquiries into this murder…

ANNE. But, I didn't do it!

BATTLE. *(taking a deep breath)* Miss Meredith. I'd like to take your word for it. But, it isn't possible and I'm sure you understand that. *(then)* You left Mrs. Eldon when she went abroad…

ANNE. *(cutting in)* Yes, that's right. I went to live in Devon. I worked for Rhoda's aunt. Mrs. Deering.

BATTLE. *(making a note of this)* Thank you. I knew you went to Devon but I hadn't traced the name of your employer there. So. In the past three years you've had two jobs?

ANNE. *(hesitating)* Yes. I would have still been in Devon but, unfortunately Mrs. Deering died – of cancer. I suppose you could say Rhoda took pity on me and offered me a home here. I've no money of my own, you see.

BATTLE. I did know.

ANNE. *(looking at him resentfully)* I can't help being – poor.

BATTLE. Forgive me for saying this, but it doesn't seem to inhibit you.

ANNE. I have a very small annuity left me by my father. And I am Rhoda's "paid" companion – as well as being her friend.

BATTLE. And I don't suppose you live riotously here in the country.

ANNE. That's how I managed to save for my trip to Switzerland.

BATTLE. Where you met Shaitana.

ANNE. I got nothing from him.

BATTLE. How exactly *did* you meet him?

ANNE. *(after a slight pause)* Rhoda introduced us. I think she was matchmaking. Trying to find me a rich husband. But I didn't care for him in that way.

BATTLE. But, you liked him, nevertheless.

ANNE. He took me to dinner – quite often. If you want to know what *he* got out of the relationship – well, he was aware of Rhoda and the others trying to pair us off and he played up to it. It amused him to hint – certain things about him and me. Gave the others something to gossip about. They used to giggle in corners.

BATTLE. You didn't care for Shaitana amusing himself that way?

ANNE. No. *(then bitterly)* But beggars can't be choosers.

BATTLE. I'm sorry, but I must ask this. Did he seduce you?

ANNE. *(springing to her feet)* He most certainly did not.

(a moment)

BATTLE. That'll be all for now, Miss Meredith. You may or may not know…

(He waits for a reaction from the irate ANNE.)

… that Shaitana had a nasty habit of digging into people's private lives. If anything occurs to you – something that may have slipped your mind – that he could have uncovered…

ANNE. I've told you everything.

(BATTLE nods acceptance then, without a word, he turns and exits.)

(ANNE, clearly agitated, watches him go.)

(a moment)

(RHODA returns through the french windows. She carries a letter.)

RHODA. He's gone then.

(ANNE turns to her.)

The afternoon post has arrived. There's one for you.

(She hands the letter to **ANNE**, *who looks at it.)*

RHODA. Recognize the writing?

ANNE. No. *(She opens the letter and reads it to herself.)*

RHODA. Not bad news, I hope.

ANNE. *(looking up)* No. It's from Mrs. Lorrimer. She was at the – dinner party. Asking me to call next time I'm in London.

RHODA. That's nice.

(a moment)

ANNE. I wonder why.

RHODA. Anne. I've got to say this. I couldn't help overhearing just now. Why did you lie to Superintendent Battle?

(The lights fade down on Wendon Lodge. **ANNE** *and* **RHODA** *exit.)*

*(***O'CONNOR** *enters* **SHAITANA**'s *drawing-room and sits at the card table and studies his notepad.)*

(The lights fade up on **SHAITANA**'s *drawing-room.)*

(The door opens and **BATTLE** *enters.)*

BATTLE. Right, Sergeant. I want to know what you've found out.

O'CONNOR. Well, sir. I caught up with the person we wanted to question at the *Willy Nilly Revue Club.*

BATTLE. Enjoyed yourself, I hope.

O'CONNOR. Oh, yes, sir. I mean, no, sir. Even though our approach was meant to be unofficial I didn't take any liberties, Of course, it was necessary for me to buy Elsie...

BATTLE. Elsie?

O'CONNOR. Miss Batt, sir. I bought her a drink.

BATTLE. *(long suffering)* I'll clear that for you.

O'CONNOR. Actually, sir – it was two or three.

BATTLE. It had better be good.

O'CONNOR. I, er – engaged the young lady in conversation in the bar during the interval. I let it be known that I had worked for the Craddocks prior to their move to Mayfair. I hinted that I'd heard strange rumours after I'd left their service. Playing it very cautiously…

BATTLE. You should have been on the stage, Sergeant.

O'CONNOR. Apparently – misinformed or otherwise – Mr. Craddock was of the opinion that Dr. Roberts and Mrs. Craddock were – well, you know…

BATTLE. I'm not a girl guide, Sergeant.

O'CONNOR. Having a sexual relationship, sir.

BATTLE. And I was beginning to worry about him not being married.

O'CONNOR. Mr. Craddock threatened to tell the General Medical Council.

BATTLE. *That's* what I was hoping to hear.

O'CONNOR. I must point out, sir, that Miss Batt doesn't believe the doctor was anything other than a model gentleman. As I understand it, Mrs. Craddock made all the running. She was constantly making demands on the doctor who was at his wits end. He just didn't know how to deal with the situation.

BATTLE. Are you saying you think he was entirely innocent?

O'CONNOR. I'm telling you the facts, sir. That's what you asked me to do.

BATTLE. Dammit, Sergeant. Haven't you found out anything that could be used as evidence?

O'CONNOR. Nothing that would stand up in court, sir, especially as Mr. Craddock died from anthrax. But, there is one thing, sir. Dr. Roberts did see Mrs. Craddock just prior to her leaving for Egypt. The day before she boarded the *Oriana,* he gave her the necessary injections.

BATTLE. That has to be it.

O'CONNOR. She was alive and well when they docked in Alexandria.

BATTLE. Oh, well. Was there anything in that rumour about Major Despard shooting Professor Luxmore when they were on that expedition to South America?

O'CONNOR. It's difficult, sir.

BATTLE. Oh?

O'CONNOR. Well, although I'm pretty certain the professor died from gunshot wounds and not the yellow fever – we'd have a hard job proving it.

BATTLE. In your opinion, Sergeant.

O'CONNOR. With respect, sir, I think I'm right. When I spoke to Mrs. Luxmore she insisted that the major was madly in love with her, and that he'd shot the professor so that they could be together.

BATTLE. For goodness sake, Sergeant. This is just the sort of evidence we're looking for.

O'CONNOR. Yes, sir. Except that she'd changed her mind with her very next sentence, and inside half an hour there were five different versions of what actually happened – and why. Mrs. Luxmore is a bit of a romantic, I'm afraid.

BATTLE. Not very good in the witness box, eh?

O'CONNOR. Not as far as we're concerned, sir. How did you get on, sir?

BATTLE. *(sighing)* About the same as you. Miss Meredith appears to be poor but honest.

O'CONNOR. And Mrs. Lorrimer?

(a moment)

BATTLE. The only thing I've been able to discover about her is that she's an excellent bridge player, and I already knew that.

O'CONNOR. Nothing in her past at all?

BATTLE. Not worth bothering about.

O'CONNOR. Perhaps she's got *something* to hide?

BATTLE. She seems to have hidden it – very well indeed.

O'CONNOR. By the way, sir, the tail you put on Major Despard. He followed him to Wendon Lodge.

BATTLE. I wonder what the major's up to?

O'CONNOR. Mrs. Oliver was there too, sir.

BATTLE. Well, I did know she was going to do a bit of "private detecting."

You never know, she may come up with something useful. O'Connor Let's hope that's all she was up to, sir.

BATTLE. Why, do you suspect her?

O'CONNOR. Put it this way, sir. If I was the murderer, I might well offer to help the police out. That way I could control things to a certain extent. Create all manner of red herrings. And if any clues turned up that were likely to lead in my direction... I'd make damned sure they were redirected – up a blind alley.

BATTLE. You don't trust anyone, do you Sergeant?

O'CONNOR. *(putting his notepad away)* With respect, sir, it's something I learned from an expert.

BATTLE. Who?

O'CONNOR. You, sir. At one of your lectures. I remember you were most adamant about it. "Don't even trust your own grandmother when it comes to murder," you said.

BATTLE. Did I?

O'CONNOR. Yes, sir.

BATTLE. Yes, well, it's a very good principle to stand by, Sergeant.

O'CONNOR. Yes, sir.

(The phone rings and gets **BATTLE** *"off the hook." The phone rings again and* **O'CONNOR** *coughs and moves towards the phone but* **BATTLE** *stops him.)*

BATTLE. I'll answer it. *(He does so.)* Superintendent Battle... Speak up, I can't hear you... *(a longish pause)...* Are you certain?... Who is this?... Blast they've hung up. *(He replaces the receiver.)*

O'CONNOR. What is it, sir?

BATTLE. *(after a slight pause)* It was before your time, Sergeant, but there was a very famous murder case in New York in nineteen hundred and ten. Edward Stanford – a wealthy American industrialist – was found dead in an East Side apartment. It hit the headlines over here because his wife was English and she disappeared without trace.

O'CONNOR. *(after a slight pause)* Has it got something to do with this case, sir?

BATTLE. *(indicating the phone)* I've just been told that Mrs. Stanford is alive and well and living in London under the name of Mrs. Lorrimer.

(curtain)

ACT II

Scene I

*(**MRS. LORRIMER** drawing-room. A week later.)*

*(It is set in exactly the same area as **SHAITANA** drawing-room in Act I with a door upstage center and french windows right as before and will need to be cleverly disguised to convey the impression of a completely different room. In the London production this was helped by using furniture of the art deco style to contrast sharply with that used for **SHAITANA**'s room. There is a sofa with two armchairs, a coffee table and occasional table, a writing desk and stool and two winged chairs. Table lamps, ornaments and vases of flowers are arranged on the cabinets and bookcase.)*

*(As the curtain rises **MRS. LORRIMER** is seated on the sofa pouring tea from a tray on the coffee table. She hands a cup to **ANNE** who is standing nearby.)*

MRS. LORRIMER. I do hope you didn't come up to town especially.

ANNE. Oh, no. *(She takes her tea to the armchar right and sits.)* I mean, I could have. I was very pleased to get your letter. It cheered me up no end.

But, the truth is, I had to come up to see a solicitor anyway.

MRS. LORRIMER. *(with eyebrows raised)* You feel in need of legal advice, do you?

ANNE. It was Major Despard's idea.

MRS. LORRIMER. How strange.

ANNE. I think it was only because he thought I was alone in the world.

63

MRS. LORRIMER. Where you're concerned, my dear, there may have been more to it. You're very attractive. But, what's puzzling is, he also came to me and suggested the same thing.

ANNE. That is odd.

MRS. LORRIMER. Very. Of course, I didn't need his advice. I have a perfectly good solicitor. But, it does make one wonder what that man is up to.

ANNE. I don't think he would do anything dishonourable.

(**MRS. LORRIMER** *is about to say something but stops herself and smiles.*)

MRS. LORRIMER. Yes, I expect you're right. I'm just being cautious. And, I'm worried about you, too, my dear. Because you're alone really, aren't you?

ANNE. Both my parents are dead. But, 1 have lots of friends.

MRS. LORRIMER. I never had children, so, now I'm alone too. *(then)* However, I didn't ask you here to talk about me.

ANNE. I don't mind. I enjoy hearing about other people's lives.

MRS. LORRIMER. Mine is far too dull to go in to. *(then)* Has Superintendent Battle been to see you?

ANNE. *(shooting a worried glance)* He came all the way down to Walling-ford. It was so unnecessary. *(then)* Um – has he been to see you?

MRS. LORRIMER. I haven't seen him since that evening.

ANNE. I thought he was questioning everyone.

MRS. LORRIMER. Perhaps I don't look like a murderer... *(But even as she says it, she realizes it doesn't sound too good.)*

ANNE. Oh...

MRS. LORRIMER. Forgive me. I wasn't implying that you do. But, I'm an old woman.

ANNE. You mustn't say that about yourself. *(She puts her cup down on the occasional table.)*

MRS. LORRIMER. The best has gone. *(then)* How old are you, Anne?

ANNE. Twenty-five.

MRS. LORRIMER. You should be married.

ANNE. Everyone's trying to marry me off – preferably to a rich husband.

MRS. LORRIMER. Be very careful.

(a moment)

ANNE. Mrs. Lorrimer. Who do you think killed Mr. Shaitana?

*(For a moment **MRS. LORRIMER** is thrown off guard. But, she quickly composes herself.)*

MRS. LORRIMER. You really are worried about it, aren't you?

ANNE. You must have given it some thought.

MRS. LORRIMER. A little.

ANNE. But, *surely* you've got a theory.

(a moment)

MRS. LORRIMER. Anne. You think Superintendent Battle suspects you, don't you?

ANNE. *(nervously)* Well, he seems to be paying me an awful lot of attention.

Much more so than anyone else.

MRS. LORRIMER. *(after a slight pause)* You're not hiding anything, Anne?

*(There's just a flicker of reaction, barely noticeable, from **ANNE.**)*

ANNE. Why me?

MRS. LORRIMER. Calm down, dear. It's simply that in my experience the police are like a dog with a bone if they believe that someone has something to hide.

ANNE. I haven't.

MRS. LORRIMER. Then you have nothing to worry about. That's the point I was making.

ANNE. *(after a slight pause)* D'you think they'll ever find the murderer?

MRS. LORRIMER. Come along, child. This is much too morbid a subject.

ANNE. I'm sorry. I just have this terrible feeling. I can't shake it off. And last night – I had this nightmare – my hands were tied – the noose was around my neck – I heard the lever pulled, I…

MRS. LORRIMER. Anne, Anne, stop it! *(She crosses to ANNE.)*

(ANNE breaks down. MRS. LORRIMER takes her by the shoulders.)

Listen to me. I'm sure something will happen – to clear you of the murder. It doesn't matter what you've done – it *will* happen. When that happens you'll have nothing to worry about. You'll be safe.

(a moment)

When it's all over. When you're safe. I want you to promise me you'll never do anything – wrong again.

(She helps ANNE up.)

Promise me.

ANNE. I promise.

MRS. LORRIMER. Whatever you do – don't let me down.

(But somehow we get the feeling ANNE won't stick to it. She turns away as the Lights fade to blackout.)

(ANNE and MRS. LORRIMER exit.)

(MRS. OLIVER and RHODA enter the flat set. MRS. OLIVER sits on the swivel stool and RHODA on the upright chair.)

(The Lights fade up on MRS. OLIVER's flat, left. There is a desk center with a swivel stool in front and a waste-paper basket by the side of it. Pictures hang on the wall above and there are books strewn around the floor and on the stool left. There are more books on the shelves right

and an upright chair set below them. A cardboard box, containing eighteen packets of stockings and one pair loose, is propped against the leg of the desk right.)

(MRS. OLIVER is holding out the bag of apples to RHODA.)

RHODA. Oh, no thank you. I couldn't. Three's enough.

(MRS. OLIVER takes a large Cox's apple out of the bag. She bites into the apple, clearly enjoying herself.)

MRS. OLIVER. I never stop eating them when I'm working.

RHODA. I'm not interrupting, am I?

MRS. OLIVER. I never stop eating them when I'm not working. Anyway, I'll do anything to get away from the typewriter.

(RHODA laughs.)

RHODA. *(checking her watch)* Anne should be here soon if we are going to catch our train.

MRS. OLIVER. With Major Despard, is she?

RHODA. Yes, he's taking her to see his solicitor, and then she was going to pop in on Mrs. Lorrimer.

MRS. OLIVER. I wonder why he arranged that?

RHODA. He wants to help her.

MRS. OLIVER. I don't know that it is a help. In fact, it makes her look more guilty. Still, perhaps that's what he wants.

RHODA. Oh, no! He's such a nice man – upright...

MRS. OLIVER. Handsome?

RHODA. Well, er – I suppose he is.

MRS. OLIVER. Have you fallen for him?

RHODA. What a question.

MRS. OLIVER. My dear, at my age it's the sort of question you can ask and not even turn a hair. And, I grant you, he's a good looking specimen.

RHODA. I think he's more interested in Anne.

(a moment)

MRS. OLIVER. How well do you know her?

RHODA. *(looking up in surprise)* Well, I… We share the same house…

MRS. OLIVER. It's true, you've got to live with someone to know them really well – but, the truth is – you *don't* know her that well, do you?

RHODA. Are you saying I'm naive?

MRS. OLIVER. Look, I'm not trying to be offensive. I like you. But, I think you're too trusting.

RHODA. I know Anne was rude to you the other day, but I really believe it was only because of all this business. It's put her under an awful strain. I'm sure she didn't mean to upset you.

MRS. OLIVER. Rhoda, if I ever need a really good friend, I'd like it to be you.

RHODA. *(embarrassed)* You are kind.

MRS. OLIVER. Not at all. Be careful, my dear.

RHODA. There is one thing that's been worrying me…

MRS. OLIVER. D'you want to tell me about it?

RHODA. Well, I… Anne might be angry with me if I do.

MRS. OLIVER. I won't tell her.

RHODA. Well… It was when she was in Devon.

MRS. OLIVER. As companion to your aunt?

RHODA. No. Before that.

MRS. OLIVER. I thought she came straight from the Isle of Wight to the job with Mrs. Deering.

RHODA. Well, no. Not exactly. She had another job. Only for three weeks though. That's why she hasn't said anything about it. She thought it didn't count.

MRS. OLIVER. Well, it was only three weeks.

RHODA. I suppose you're right.

MRS. OLIVER. And, if your aunt was offering her a better job.

RHODA. Oh, it wasn't that.

MRS. OLIVER. No?

RHODA. Oh, no. The person she was with – Mrs. Benson – died.

(A moment; **MRS. OLIVER** *stares at* **RHODA.***)*

MRS. OLIVER. What did she die of?

RHODA. She was poisoned.

(another moment)

It was horrible. For everyone. She died in agony.

MRS. OLIVER. *(gathering her thoughts)* But, how was she poisoned?

RHODA. She drank some hat paint.

MRS. OLIVER. Hat paint! That's lethal stuff.

RHODA. Absolutely. She mistook it for medicine. *(then)* It was all her own fault. She'd asked Anne to paint an old garden hat black. When she'd finished she unfortunately broke the neck of the bottle. Mrs. Benson told her to pour the paint into an old syrup of figs bottle. The servants all heard her saying it. Then, somehow the two bottles got mixed up and, well – I've told you what happened. *(then)* I think Anne feels partly responsible.

MRS. OLIVER. Yes…

RHODA. Of course, it was an accident.

MRS. OLIVER. Tragic.

RHODA. Poor Anne. Still I do think she should have told Superintendent Battle about it.

MRS. OLIVER. He'll find out.

RHODA. That's what I said. But, she insists that by the time he does they'll have found the murderer and it won't matter.

MRS. OLIVER. Unless…

RHODA. Yes?

MRS. OLIVER. *(smiling)* Oh, nothing. It's the writer in me coming out. I've got an evil mind, you know.

(They both enjoy this remark.)

Let's talk about something else. I love that dress you're wearing.

RHODA. Thank you.

MRS. OLIVER. You've both got good taste. Anne dresses extremely well.

RHODA. Yes, nice subtle colours.

MRS. OLIVER. Expensive. How does she do it?

RHODA. Oh... Well... I don't charge her any rent, of course – we're friends. I suppose she must have a little money of her own. I've never asked. *(then)* Mrs. Oliver. You haven't changed the subject, have you?

MRS. OLIVER. *(after a slight pause)* I'm sorry. But, doesn't it ever bother you where Anne gets the money from to do all the things that well-off people do?

*(**RHODA** is about to answer but, the front doorbell rings.)*

Ah, I wonder if that's her now? *(She gets up to answer the door.)*

RHODA. By the way. I've lent her some money. She's promised to pay me back when she's sorted out.

*(**MRS. OLIVER** exits without a word.)*

MRS. OLIVER. *(off)* Ah, there you are, dear. Won't you come in?

(a moment)

*(**ANNE** enters followed by **MRS. OLIVER**.)*

ANNE. *(to **RHODA**)* Not too late am I? For the five-fifteen?

RHODA. We'll be all right, darling. How did it go?

ANNE. He seems a very competent man. *(then, with feeling)* I'm not to talk to anyone about it unless he's there.

*(It doesn't pass unnoticed. There is a slight awkward moment which **MRS. OLIVER** breaks.)*

MRS. OLIVER. Would you like a Cox's? *(She produces an apple from her pocket.)*

ANNE. *(taken by surprise)* Oh, er – no thank you. I really couldn't eat anything.

MRS. OLIVER. Upsetting, was it? At the solicitor's?

ANNE. No. *(to* **RHODA***)* Perhaps we ought to be going, Rhoda.

RHODA. Well – yes.

MRS. OLIVER. Oh. What a pity. I was so enjoying your company.

RHODA. I've had a lovely time. Thank you.

MRS. OLIVER. Do come again. Just before you go, I wonder if you'd mind helping me? *(She picks up the stocking box.)* Have I ever told you I've got eight nieces?

RHODA. *(shaking her head)* No...

MRS. OLIVER. Well, I have. The thing is, every Christmas I send each one of them a pair of silk stockings. Well, I rang Harvey Nichols this morning and they sent round this boxful. Just in from Paris.

(She opens the box and puts it on top of the typewriter.)

ANNE. *(looking into the box)* Goodness! How many pairs are there?

MRS. OLIVER. I've no idea. They told me to choose eight pairs and send the rest back. I can't make up my mind. I was rather hoping you would both help me. After all, you're the same generation, and, it'll only take a moment.

*(***ANNE** *is already dipping into the box, and* **RHODA** *does too.)*

ANNE. *(excitedly)* They're all gorgeous. *(She holds out a packet to* **MRS. OLIVER.***)* I love these. They're almost silver.

MRS. OLIVER. *(taking them)* That'll be one pair then.

RHODA. Mauve! How wonderful. And pink!

(She hands these to **MRS. OLIVER.** *This continues during the following until they have selected eight pairs.)*

ANNE. They're *pure* silk.

MRS. OLIVER. Thirty-eight and sixpence a pair!

RHODA. Gosh! Your nieces are very lucky.

MRS. OLIVER. I agree. They've got a lovely aunt.

ANNE. These three pairs are delicious.

RHODA. *(taking two packets to* MRS. OLIVER*)* I like these two. I like them all!

*(*RHODA *and* MRS. OLIVER *move downstage and, as* MRS. OLIVER *speaks,* ANNE *steals two packets of stockings from the box.)*

MRS. OLIVER. Well, I've got my eight pairs now. And thank you both.

RHODA. Thank you! I enjoyed myself.

ANNE. *(moving towards the door)* I think we ought to be going, Rhoda.

RHODA. Pity.

MRS. OLIVER. I'll see you out.

ANNE. There's no need. We can find our way. Goodbye, Mrs. Oliver.

MRS. OLIVER. Goodbye, my dears. Safe journey.

*(*ANNE *and* RHODA *exit.)*

(as a parting shot) Rhoda, take care. *(A moment, then she starts to count the stockings, starting with the eight the girls have chosen.)* Eight. Ten. Twelve. Fourteen. Sixteen. *(after a slight pause)* Seventeen...

(The lights fade to blackout on MRS. OLIVER*'s flat.)*

*(*MRS. OLIVER *exits.)*

*(*ROBERTS *and* MRS. LORRIMER *enter the drawing-room.)*

(The lights fade up on MRS. LORRIMER *and* ROBERTS*. She is sitting at her desk, writing. He is standing nearby holding a cup of tea – the one* ANNE *left on the occasional table.)*

MRS. LORRIMER. Do forgive me, Dr. Roberts. But, whatever I do, I must get *this* letter in the post by this evening.

ROBERTS. Don't apologize. First things first.

(She finishes off writing her letter and places it into an envelope. Then she crosses and sits in the armchair.)

MRS. LORRIMER. Now. You have my undivided attention.

ROBERTS. *(after a slight pause)* I've been asked to play bridge for the County of Middlesex.

MRS. LORRIMER. That's quite an honour. Congratulations.

ROBERTS. Thank you. Unfortunately, my practice is so demanding I can't fit it in.

MRS. LORRIMER. *Surely* you can arrange something.

ROBERTS. The match takes place over the Easter weekend next year. It would be easy enough for me to get one day off – possibly two – but four days that particular weekend is out of the question.

MRS. LORRIMER. Oh, come now, Doctor. You've plenty of time to find a locum.

ROBERTS. That's not all. Practice matches have been arranged every weekend from Christmas on. I can't give them a guarantee that I shall be available.

MRS. LORRIMER. Why have you come to see me about it, Doctor?

ROBERTS. I think you know. *(He puts the tea cup on the tray. Then.)* The Selection Committee has asked me to suggest someone to take my place. I had no hesitation in putting your name forward.

(a moment)

MRS. LORRIMER. I'm very sorry, Dr. Roberts. I shall be unable to accept.

ROBERTS. *(after a slight pause)* They will be disappointed. Are you sure you won't be available?

MRS. LORRIMER. I'm afraid – I won't be here.

ROBERTS. Oh. Going abroad?

MRS. LORRIMER. And I shan't be returning.

(a moment)

ROBERTS. Well, can't say I blame you. The weather in this country's positively bronchial. It'll be far better for your health.

(There is a searching moment.)

MRS. LORRIMER. Quite.

ROBERTS. Well. If you won't – or can't change your mind…

MRS. LORRIMER. My mind is made up, Doctor.

ROBERTS. *(nodding)* Yes.

MRS. LORRIMER. However, thank you for considering me a good enough player to represent the County.

ROBERTS. My dear, Mrs. Lorrimer, we both know you're a far better player than I could ever be. It just so happens that the Chairman of the Selection Committee is an old friend.

MRS. LORRIMER. You're far too modest. *(She gets up.)* Goodbye.

(He offers her his hand and they shake hands.)

ROBERTS. Take care of yourself.

MRS. LORRIMER. There's no need to worry about me.

(Then he notices the letter on the desk.)

ROBERTS. Oh, er – would you like me to post your letter?

MRS. LORRIMER. I still have more to write. My maid will do it.

ROBERTS. It's no bother.

MRS. LORRIMER. Very well.

(He picks up the letter.)

ROBERTS. Goodbye then. And let's hope this murder business resolves itself soon.

MRS. LORRIMER. It will.

ROBERTS. We both know who did it, don't we?

MRS. LORRIMER. Do we?

ROBERTS. Yes, I'm sure we do. I *saw* it happen. And I think you did too.

(The lights fade to blackout on **MRS. LORRIMER'S** *drawing-room.)*

*(***ROBERTS** *and* **MRS. LORRIMER** *exit.)*

*(***BATTLE** *and* **ROBERTS** *enter the flat set.)*

(The lights come up on **MRS. OLIVER** *flat.* **BATTLE** *perches on the desk, holding the phone in one hand and a half-chewed apple in the other. Clearly, he doesn't know what to do with the apple.* **MRS. OLIVER** *sits in the upright chair eating an apple.)*

BATTLE. *(into the receiver)* No, that's fine. Absolutely fine, Inspector. But, if anything else occurs to you don't hesitate to contact me. Goodbye.

(He replaces the phone and looks around for somewhere to put the chewed apple. **MRS. OLIVER** *watches him and he reluctantly takes a little bite.)*

(swallowing) Well.

MRS. OLIVER. Delicious, aren't they?

BATTLE. *(weakly)* Yes. *(He drops the apple in the waste-paper basket.)* The thing is, the Combeacre police confirm that it was an accident.

MRS. OLIVER. Rubbish.

BATTLE. They read the report over to me. They seem very efficient.

MRS. OLIVER. Bunch of yokels.

BATTLE. You're talking about my colleagues, Mrs. Oliver.

MRS. OLIVER. After this, I shouldn't think you'd want your name linked with them.

BATTLE. *(shaking his head)* I don't know why I let you get away with this. I must be getting soft. The inquest produced a verdict of accidental death... Two of Mrs. Benson's servants – the cook and the maid – both overheard her telling Miss Meredith to put the paint in the syrup of figs bottle *and* place it on top of the bathroom cabinet.

MRS. OLIVER. Silly woman. She made it so easy for her.

BATTLE. Be very careful who you say things like that to. And, what about your main contender, Dr. Roberts?

MRS. OLIVER. Mmmm. Yes. The joker in the pack. He's still in the running. I haven't totally given him up.

BATTLE. Well, they couldn't all have done it.

MRS. OLIVER. A conspiracy?

(BATTLE *is about to protest.*)

Before you dismiss it out of hand, remember that Shaitana had them all marked down as murderers. What's to have stopped them all getting together before the night he was stabbed and working out a way to do it so that they'd all be suspect, but none of them could be proved guilty?

(a moment)

(*We can see from* BATTLE'S *face that he thinks it's possible.*)

BATTLE. Could they have? I mean, seriously.

MRS. OLIVER. It's a possibility, isn't it?

BATTLE. No, no, no. They didn't know each other.

MRS. OLIVER. So they say.

BATTLE. *(after a slight pause)* No! I've got to dismiss the thought. Drive it out of my mind – before it drives me mad.

MRS. OLIVER. *(getting up)* Anyway. I've got something to show you which may explain my see-saw attitude with regard to the murderers. (*She gets the box of stockings and hands it to* BATTLE.*)

BATTLE. *(rather gingerly picking up a packet)* Silk stockings? (*He examines the packet a little closer*) Good Lord! Thirty-eight and sixpence a pair! It's almost a constable's pay for a week.

MRS. OLIVER. I don't suppose a police constable has any occasion to either buy or wear silk stockings.

BATTLE. Well, what is their significance?

MRS. OLIVER. Count them.

(**BATTLE** *quickly counts them in the box.*)

BATTLE. Seventeen pairs. A small fortune.

MRS. OLIVER. I've been very clever, Superintendent.

BATTLE. D'you know, I don't honestly think that modesty would sit very well on your shoulders, Mrs. Oliver.

MRS. OLIVER. I agree. *(after a pause)* Hear me out. Earlier this afternoon, I asked Anne Meredith and Rhoda Dawes to help me choose eight pairs. Before they dipped into that box there were nineteen pairs.

BATTLE. I see.

MRS. OLIVER. Ann Meredith stole two pairs.

BATTLE. It could have been Rhoda Dawes.

MRS. OLIVER. Nonsense!

BATTLE. *(defensively)* All right. I won't argue. But, what has stealing two pairs of stockings got to do with Shaitana's death? *(He puts the box down.)*

MRS. OLIVER. Did the inspector at Combeacre say anything about Mrs. Benson's money. I mean, who got it?

BATTLE. If you think Anne Meredith murdered Mrs. Benson because she was in her will…

MRS. OLIVER. *(interrupting)* I don't. But, I asked myself this: if Anne Meredith didn't gain financially by Mrs. Benson's death – how did she gain?

(*A moment;* **BATTLE** *mulls this thought over.*)

BATTLE. I get your drift. If Anne Meredith stole from Mrs. Benson and was caught doing it – then she might very well switch the syrup of figs with the bottle of hat paint.

MRS. OLIVER. A highly-toxic substance. If so – it was murder. And that's what Shaitana meant. She murdered Mrs. Benson – and got away with it.

BATTLE. *(after a slight pause)* There's no way we can prove it.

MRS. OLIVER. She stole my stockings.

BATTLE. *(picking up the pair of loose stockings from the box)* If your theory's right – and she murdered Mrs. Benson so she wouldn't be exposed as a thief, then don't let her know about the stockings. Or you could be next on the list.

(He walks menacingly towards MRS. OLIVER *with the stockings in his hand.)*

(a moment)

(The phone rings.)

MRS. OLIVER. *(answering the phone)* Two-four-seven-eight… *(handing the phone to Battle)* It's for you.

BATTLE. Oh, thank you. *(on the phone)* Battle here… I see. I'll call in on my way back. Any other messages, Sergeant?… OK, thank you.
Goodbye. *(He replaces the receiver.)* Mrs. Lorrimer has asked to see me urgently. She told my sergeant she knows who murdered Shaitana.

(The Lights fade to blackout on MRS. OLIVER'S *flat.)*

*(*BATTLE *and* MRS. OLIVER *exit.)*

*(*MRS. LORRIMER *enters the drawing-room.)*

(The lights fade up on MRS. LORRIMER'S *drawing-room.)*

*(*MRS. LORRIMER *is in the armchair right, dozing. She has a glass of whisky on the table beside her.)*

*(*DORIS, *the maid, enters, goes to* MRS. LORRIMER, *and gently touches her to wake her up.)*

*(*MRS. LORRIMER *sits up.)*

DORIS. I'm sorry to disturb you, mum, but Superintendent Battle's here to see you.

(There is a very quick pause.)

*(*BATTLE *enters and* DORIS *exits.)*

MRS. LORRIMER. Ah, Superintendent, come and sit down.

BATTLE. *(going and sitting on the sofa)* Thank you.

MRS. LORRIMER. Can I get you something? It's rather late for tea, but I do have a very fine old malt whisky.

BATTLE. *(smiling)* No, thank you. *(after a slight pause)* I understand you have something *important* to tell me?

MRS. LORRIMER. I always think it's a mistake to rush into confidences, don't you? And good whisky should be savoured.

BATTLE. You saw Anne Meredith earlier on.

MRS. LORRIMER. Have you been spying on me, Superintendent?

BATTLE. I have to know everything about everyone involved in this business.

MRS. LORRIMER. *(after a slight pause)* Not everything. *(then)* But, I'm sure you've paid me rather a lot of attention without being too obvious. Indeed the fact that you appear to have left me alone alerted my suspicions.

BATTLE. I treated you the same as everyone else. I said to myself that Mrs. Lorrimer murdered Shaitana. *(A moment, as he waits for a reaction and gets nothing.)* And that's where I started with everyone involved. I then, of course, tried to find a motive why each of you could have done it.

MRS. LORRIMER. So, you dug very deeply into my past.

BATTLE. Not just yours. But, I'll be perfectly frank. I realized right from the start, and Mrs. Oliver was quick to confirm my view with her character breakdown based on your expertise at playing bridge...

MRS. LORRIMER. That woman is very quick to confirm anything that takes suspicion away from her.

BATTLE. Don't you want to hear what she said?

MRS. LORRIMER. I'm sure you're going to tell me. But I can guess what it will be.

BATTLE. She said you were the most intelligent suspect, the one with the coolest temperament, and the most logical powers of reasoning. Consequently, if I was forced to bet on any one person *planning* and getting away with murder – my money would go on you.

(a moment)

MRS. LORRIMER. Am I supposed to take that as a compliment?

BATTLE. For a crime to be committed *successfully* it's necessary to work out every detail beforehand – the timing must be absolutely right. The planning scrupulously correct. Each detail meticulously thought out. *(then)* Dr. Roberts might easily bungle a murder by – overcalling his hand. Major Despard would most certainly kill if necessary – but he might be far too prudent to commit murder. Miss Meredith could easily become frightened, and give herself away…

MRS. LORRIMER. And I?

BATTLE. *You* Mrs. Lorrimer are the kind of person who could commit the perfect murder. *(after a slight pause)* If it was *planned.* But, there is another type of person who could be equally successful. Have you ever said suddenly to anyone: "Throw a stone and see if you can hit that tree?" The person does so – without thinking – and more often than not, hits the tree. On the other hand, try to get the same person to repeat the action and it's not so easy. Because he or she has started to think, to plan it, you might say. A crime committed on the spur of the moment is sometimes – inspirational. A flash of genius. No time to think. I believe it was this kind of action that led to Shaitana being murdered. And that's not your way at all. If you'd murdered Shaitana it would have been premeditated.

(a moment)

MRS. LORRIMER. And yet, Superintendent – I did murder him.

(a moment)

BATTLE. Why did you kill him, Mrs. Lorrimer?

MRS. LORRIMER. I think you know that, Superintendent.

BATTLE. Because you committed a similar crime – a long time ago?

(MRS. LORRIMER *doesn't reply. She simply bows her head in acceptance.*)

Were Shaitana's remarks at dinner aimed at you?

MRS. LORRIMER. *(raising her head)* Yes, they were. *(after a slight pause)* He'd broached the subject on other occasions – but, never so directly as the other evening. I could see the devil in his eyes as he looked at me. Taunting. Teasing. Then I asked myself: why had he invited you? Was it merely to indulge in his own cleverness? To savour the fact that he could prove I had committed a terrible crime all those years ago and *you* had no idea of it? Or was it more sinister? Was he actually going to tell you, or if not actually come out with it – at least give you a clue? I decided I couldn't take the risk. And, I knew, I had to do something about it.

BATTLE. That's what interests me. When? The exact moment, please – that you decided that Shaitana had to be silenced forever?

MRS. LORRIMER. I'd seen the dagger before we went into dinner. When we returned to the drawing-room my eyes were constantly drawn to it. I can't say exactly when I decided to do what I did. I knew I was taking a risk but I thought it was worth it.

BATTLE. You weighed up your chances, did you?

MRS. LORRIMER. We started to play bridge. Then the opportunity suddenly came my way. I was dummy. I strolled across to the fireplace even while I was poking the fire my eyes were riveted on the dagger. Mercifully, Shaitana was asleep. A quick look across at the others. The dagger was up my sleeve. I hesitated – it was now or never. Then I leaned over him. Even so, I was torn – it was an agonizing moment. *Then – (She leans forward.)* – I stabbed him!

(a moment)

MRS. LORRIMER. I decided to speak to him. I thought it would help me – with an alibi. I made some asinine remark about the fire, and pretended he'd answered me so I could speak to him again.

BATTLE. Did he cry out – when you did it?

MRS. LORRIMER. That surprised me. It was just a grunt – that's all. Nothing more. It could easily have been mistaken for him actually speaking to me. Then I went back to the bridge table. The last trick was being played.

BATTLE. There's something bothering me. *(then)* You decide to take what can only be described as an enormous risk. What's more, it actually pays off. You actually get away with murder.

(She shoots him a quick surprised glance.)

Oh, yes, indeed, Mrs. Lorrimer. I would find it very hard to prove you did it. However, a week later you decide to confess. It somehow doesn't quite fit in with what I know about your character.

(a moment)

*(**MRS. LORRIMER** smiles and drinks some whisky.)*

MRS. LORRIMER. When Anne Meredith was taking tea with me this afternoon, I realized I was not an entirely wicked person. There I was – calmly drinking tea with this young girl whose whole life lay ahead of her. It struck me that by my actions I was putting her life in jeopardy. I couldn't undo what I'd done. I'd murdered Shaitana and that was that. Because of this, not only Anne, but Dr. Roberts and Major Despard – none of whom had injured me in any way whatsoever – being forced to go through probably the most traumatic experience of their lives, and one of them might well be in great danger. That I could undo. Well, with this thought nagging at me I couldn't delay this meeting any longer...

(a moment)

BATTLE. No. No, I'm sorry. I can't accept what you say. The truth is, at this moment, I couldn't hang it on any one of them either. And, I think you're aware of that.

(a moment)

MRS. LORRIMER. I was rather hoping not to have to go in to this. However, you leave me no choice. This morning, I had a rather important appointment. I learned from a specialist in Harley Street – *(She smiles.)* – that I shall not be dealing many more hands. Indeed, all my cards are on the table. Face up. The top card being the ace of spades.

(a moment)

BATTLE. I'm very sorry.

MRS. LORRIMER. That's kind of you. But, you mustn't forget that I *murdered* Shaitana.

BATTLE. And you still insist you stabbed Shaitana? Without giving it more than a moment's thought?

MRS. LORRIMER. *(flatly)* Yes.

(a moment)

BATTLE. Yes. I'm quite willing to believe you murdered Shaitana. You've already suggested you did a similar thing in the past – which I shall be looking into.

MRS. LORRIMER. I understand.

BATTLE. What's more, I believe it has a distinct bearing on this meeting. I imagine that when you saw the specialist and heard the news – you were carried away with your emotions.

MRS. LORRIMER. Superintendent! I thought you had an insight into my character!

BATTLE. *(holding up a restraining hand)* Hear me out, please. You saw Anne Meredith this afternoon, and you couldn't help feeling compassion for her.

MRS. LORRIMER. That's ridiculous!

BATTLE. Because… she had done exactly what you did years ago. Mrs. Lorrimer. I want the *truth*. You saw Anne Meredith murder Shaitana – didn't you?

(blackout)

Scene II

(The same. The following morning.)

*(O'CONNOR opens the door and **BATTLE** enters, followed by **ROBERTS**. **O'CONNOR**. steps into the room, closes the door, and stands upstage left.)*

BATTLE. Now, go through it from the beginning, Doctor. Try to remember *all* the details.

ROBERTS. I'll do my best.

BATTLE. Do better than that, please.

*(It causes a slightly awkward moment but **ROBERTS** decides to ignore it.)*

ROBERTS. I got up about seven-thirty A.M. I came downstairs, and my housekeeper had prepared breakfast. Well, breakfast isn't breakfast for me if I haven't got *The Times* to read. And, it hadn't arrived. Put me in an irritable frame of mind.

BATTLE. Yes, yes.

ROBERTS. Then I thought I heard it drop through the letter-box. It turned out to be the post. I don't usually look at my letters until Miss Burgess arrives but, since I had nothing else to do, I opened one. It was from Mrs. Lorrimer. *(He takes it out of his pocket and opens it.)* Briefly, it says *(paraphrasing):* she's sorry for all the trouble she's caused us... that it was she who'd murdered Shaitana... and that it was her intention to put matters right. *(looking up)* She goes on to explain about having seen a Harley Street man and the result of that consultation.

*(He hands the letter to **BATTLE** who starts reading it.)*

I also gather she's written the same letter to Despard and Miss Meredith.

BATTLE. What did you do next?

ROBERTS. I didn't hesitate. Except to get my housekeeper to phone you.

Then I got in the car and dashed round here. I tried artificial respiration.

Heart massage. I didn't have any adrenalin with me but, in any case, it was too late.

BATTLE. *(looking up from the letter)* Overdose?

(ROBERTS hands him a small pill bottle.)

ROBERTS. Sleeping tablets. Veronal. One of the barbiturates.

(BATTLE examines the bottle.)

BATTLE. Yesterday's date on this.

ROBERTS. I did notice. She must have taken the lot.

BATTLE. Sergeant, would you ask the maid to come in, please?

(O'CONNOR exits.)

ROBERTS. Look, if you don't need me anymore I have rather a busy morning ahead of me. And, it does seem as though you've solved Shaitana's murder.

BATTLE. Yes. It does. Doesn't it?

ROBERTS. I'm sorry I couldn't have done more to help her.

BATTLE. Yes – of course. Thank you, Doctor.

(ROBERTS exits.)

(a moment)

(There is a knock on the door.)

Yes.

(O'CONNOR shows in DORIS, who is sniffing into a handkerchief, and then exits.)

(moving up to DORIS; kindly) Come and sit down, please. I realize this is distressing. But, I do need your help.

(He guides her towards the sofa.)

DORIS. Oh, sir. It's all so dreadful. So very dreadful. To think you were sitting here with her only yesterday.

BATTLE. I want you to be very brave and tell me exactly what happened this morning.

DORIS. *(perching on the edge of the sofa)* I can't. I can't go through it all.

BATTLE. *(firmly, but kindly)* Yes, you can. You've got to. For her sake.

DORIS. Oh, sir. I shall never forget this morning.

BATTLE. Start at the beginning.

DORIS. The doorbell rang three times. As though it was something urgent. I answered it. And it was the gentleman who's just gone out. He says, "Where's your mistress?" I was so taken aback I could hardly answer. You see, we never went into the mistress until she rang. I just couldn't get a word out. So he bellowed at me, "Where's her room?" And he ran upstairs with me following. Then he rushes in. Without even knocking, if you please. He took one look at her lying there and says, "Oh, Lord I think it's too late." He sends me for hot water and brandy. It was desperate, sir. He tried so hard to bring her round. But she was gone all right. I could see it was no good. But, he still wouldn't give up. *(She starts sniffing again.)*

BATTLE. Thank you. Did Mrs. Lorrimer seem at all upset last night?

DORIS. No, sir. But I could tell she was in pain. Not that she said anything. She wasn't one for complaining.

BATTLE. When I left last night Mrs. Lorrimer was going to finish some letters. Did she?

DORIS. Yes, sir.

BATTLE. What happened to them?

DORIS. She gave them to me and I put them on the hall table, so I could post them later.

BATTLE. And did you?

DORIS. *(hesitantly)* Well…

BATTLE. *(excitedly)* You mean you didn't post them?

DORIS. I was going to. Well, I wouldn't have liked the mistress to know – but it was raining. And when the gentleman offered...

BATTLE. *Which gentleman?*

DORIS. The bearded gentleman, sir.

BATTLE. Major Despard?

DORIS. Yes, sir. He called here. Quite a long while after you'd left. I tried to put him off, but he was insistent. And the mistress looked so tired.

BATTLE. *(moving quickly to the door, calling)* Sergeant.

(O'CONNOR enters.)

O'CONNOR. Sir.

BATTLE. Telephone Major Despard and tell him I want to see him here immediately.

O'CONNOR. Sir.

(O'CONNOR exits.)

BATTLE. Now. I want to know one other thing. Think very carefully. How many letters were there?

DORIS. *(after a slight pause)* Two – no I tell a lie there were three.

BATTLE. Good. Now this is crucial. Who were they addressed to?

(a moment)

DORIS. I don't know, sir.

BATTLE. Think!

DORIS. *(flustered)* I can't...

BATTLE. You must try to remember. You saw the top one.

DORIS. Yes, sir...

BATTLE. You must have seen an address on it.

DORIS. *(tremulously)* I don't remember...

BATTLE. It's *very* important.

DORIS. I didn't notice. *(then)* But, I'm sure one of them was for Harrods.

(**BATTLE** *reacts to this last remark.*)

BATTLE. How can you be sure if you didn't notice?

DORIS. Because I asked the mistress to order some things for cook and pay the bill. I saw her write out the cheque and slip it into the envelope. Then, I put the letters on the table afterwards.

BATTLE. *(sighing)* Now. Are you sure there isn't anything else you ought to tell me?

DORIS. Nothing, sir.

BATTLE. Very well. You can go now.

DORIS. Thank you, sir. *(She gets up to exit.)* Oh, I did hear a car in the night, sir.

(**BATTLE** *spins round to face her.*)

BATTLE. Right outside?

DORIS. Yes, sir. I wasn't having a very good night. It must have been about two in the morning. I thought I heard it go round the back, but I couldn't be sure. Then I heard it drive off again about half an hour later.

BATTLE. Thank you.

(She exits.)

(a moment)

(**BATTLE** *stands deep in thought. Then he springs across the room to the door.*)

(shouting) Sergeant!

(**O'CONNOR** *comes in smartly.*)

What ne devil have you been up to?

BATTLE. Has he left his flat?

O'CONNOR. According to the caretaker he went this morning. Hurled everything into his car and drove off.

BATTLE. The caretaker has no idea where he went?

O'CONNOR. None at all. Except that he drove off down Piccadilly in the direction of Green Park.

BATTLE. Probably making for Wendon Lodge. *(then)* Sergeant, I don't believe Mrs. Lorrimer wrote that suicide letter to the doctor or to Major Despard and Miss Meredith.

O'CONNOR. Someone must have forged them? And, whoever it was – is the murderer?

BATTLE. And, I tell you something else, Sergeant. Miss Dawes –

O'CONNOR. Miss Meredith's friend, sir?

BATTLE. Yes. I believe she's in great danger. Very great danger indeed.

*(**BATTLE** and **O'CONNOR** rush out of the door.)*

(blackout)

*(**ANNE** and **RHODA** enter the Wendon Lodge set.)*

*(The lights fade up on **ANNE** and **RHODA** on the patio of Wendon Lodge. They appear to be in the middle of an argument. **RHODA** is seated while **ANNE** paces about.)*

ANNE. Are you sure you haven't said anything to anyone?

RHODA. *(nervously)* Me?

ANNE. Well? *(She moves up close to **RHODA**.)* You didn't tell the superintendent, did you?

RHODA. No.

ANNE. You're not lying to me are you, Rhoda?

RHODA. I swear to you. I haven't said a word to him about Combeacre. Really, Anne. There's no need to be so thoroughly nasty.

ANNE. It's my business. If I want to tell him, I will. And, I'd rather you didn't interfere. *(She moves away.)*

RHODA. *(angrily)* I didn't tell him, damn you! What's the matter with you today? Got a guilty conscience?

(a long moment)

*(They stare angrily at each other. Then **ANNE**'s mood changes suddenly and dramatically.)*

ANNE. I'm terribly sorry, darling. I've got such an awful headache. *(She moves to* **RHODA** *and gives her a quick kiss.)* Forgive me. I can't cope. I shall be glad when it's all over.

(The anger vanishes from **RHODA***'s face.)*

RHODA. So will I.

ANNE. I need a walk to clear my head. *(then)* Why don't we go for a stroll down by the river bank.

RHODA. I've got so much to do, Anne.

ANNE. We could go out in a punt… It's very warm. I know, we could even go to The Ferry Inn. Oh, let's.

RHODA. *(hesitantly)* Oh, well…

ANNE. Oh, please. It'll be such fun.

RHODA. All right. I'll pop in and get some money. *(She gets up.)*

ANNE. Hurry.

RHODA. I'll catch you up. *(She goes to the french windows and is about to disappear, but stops.)* Oh. There's something I must ask you.

ANNE. Can't it wait?

RHODA. If I don't do it now I shall forget. Did you go out last night?

ANNE. You know I went to bed early.

RHODA. It's just that I thought I heard you go out much later. In the car.

ANNE. The car's out of action.

RHODA. No, it isn't. It's been repaired. I told you.

ANNE. Well, I didn't go out. Now, do get a move on, Rhoda.

*(***RHODA*** exits through the french windows.)*

(a moment)

*(***ANNE*** exits through the archway.)*

(a moment)

(RHODA appears through the french windows with her purse and a note pad and pen. She scribbles a quick note and leaves it by the ashtray on the table.)

ANNE. *(off)* Come along, Rhoda.

RHODA. Coming.

(She exits through the archway.)

*(Since many of us will have half-guessed what **ANNE** is up to it will help to build the tension if there is as long a pause as possible at this point.)*

*(Finally, **MAJOR DESPARD** is heard from inside the house.)*

DESPARD. *(off)* Hello there. Is anyone at home? Miss Dawes?

(He pushes open the curtain from inside the house and looks out.)

Rhoda? Anne?

*(He comes out on to the patio, looks around and then lights a cigarette. He places the match in the ashtray and doesn't see **RHODA'S** note, but, as he moves towards the windows, he catches sight of it. He reads it quickly and then puts it down on the table.)*

(He exits hurriedly through the archway.)

(a moment)

*(**O'CONNOR** appears left, round the side of the house. **BATTLE** follows him.)*

BATTLE. Sergeant, are you sure that's Despard's car?

O'CONNOR. I should know, sir.

BATTLE. Well, where is everyone?

O'CONNOR. Hopped it, sir?

BATTLE. All of them? *(He spots the note.)*

O'CONNOR. Well, it seems logical, sir.

*(**BATTLE** picks up the note and reads it.)*

What is it, sir?

BATTLE. It's from Miss Dawes. Just letting any callers know that she's gone punting with Miss Meredith. Sergeant, we may be too late!

O'CONNOR. *(pointing off right)* Look, sir. Isn't that Major Despard?

BATTLE. Good Lord! Give him a hand, man. Quick.

(O'CONNOR *rushes out through the archway.*)

(a moment)

(DESPARD *enters carrying* RHODA *who is wrapped in a car blanket. Her hair is wet and she is coughing.* O'CONNOR *follows them in and stands in the archway.*)

(indicating the chair) Bring her here. Quickly.

(DESPARD *sits on the garden chair.*)

DESPARD. *(to BATTLE)* She pushed her out of the punt.

BATTLE. Miss Meredith?

DESPARD. It over-turned. They were so close to the weir. I could only get to one of them…

BATTLE. Perhaps it's just as well.

DESPARD. Yes…

BATTLE. What made you suspect her?

DESPARD. I called on Mrs. Lorrimer last night.

BATTLE. I know.

(DESPARD *reacts, surprised.*)

DESPARD. I thought she may have seen something at Shaitana's, and I got the distinct impression she was covering for Anne – Miss Meredith. Anyway, when I left I offered to post some letters for her. I noticed one was for Harrods. Another to someone in Southampton. And the third to a doctor in Harley Street.

BATTLE. So, when you received a letter this morning…

DESPARD. I suspected it was a forgery. I knew Miss Meredith had received a letter from Mrs. Lorrimer last week, so she had plenty of time to practice forging her handwriting. I guessed it was too late to help poor Mrs. Lorrimer. But, I realized Rhoda might be next on the list. She probably knew too much, you see.

RHODA. *(weakly)* She pushed me – pushed me in.

DESPARD. You're all right now.

RHODA. She knew I couldn't swim.

DESPARD. There's nothing else to worry about. It's all over now.

BATTLE. No. I'm sorry. I'm afraid there's a few more shocks to come.

(blackout)

Scene III

(MRS. LORRIMER's drawing-room. Three hours later.)

(The lights come up.)

(ROBERTS and MRS. OLIVER enter.)

MRS. OLIVER. I don't understand, Dr. Roberts. Didn't he say anything else?

ROBERTS. No. He phoned me and explained he couldn't get hold of you...

MRS. OLIVER. But, I've been at home all day.

ROBERTS. I can only pass on what he said. He tried but got no reply and since he was in the country he asked me to get in touch with you.

MRS. OLIVER. It seems highly suspicious to me.

ROBERTS. What are you worrying about, dear lady? He probably wants to put our minds at rest.

MRS. OLIVER. He could have popped round to see me.

ROBERTS. Anyone would think you had a guilty conscience.

(MRS. OLIVER shoots him a worried glare.)

(At the same time O'CONNOR opens the door and shows in BATTLE, followed by DESPARD and RHODA. O'CONNOR comes in, closes the door and stands upstage left.)

BATTLE. Ah. Thank you both for coming.

MRS. OLIVER. *(flustered)* I've been at home all day, Superintendent. I can't understand why you couldn't get hold of me. What is this all about?

BATTLE. *(after a slight pause)* Give me a moment – please.

MRS. OLIVER. I really ought not to be here. I've got better things to do.

BATTLE. I wouldn't have asked you if it wasn't important, Mrs. Oliver.

MRS. OLIVER. In any case, you've solved it now. I always said it was that young girl, Miss Meredith. I don't know why you want me here.

BATTLE. Please sit down, and calm down, Mrs. Oliver.

(Reluctantly, MRS. OLIVER sits in the armchair right. RHODA and DESPARD sit on the sofa.)

Firstly, I'm you'll be pleased to learn that I've finished my investigations.

ROBERTS. *(going and sitting in the armchair downstage left)* What made you suspect Miss Meredith, Superintendent?

(BATTLE turns to face MRS. OLIVER who is looking very uncomfortable.)

BATTLE. It was Mrs. Oliver. She discovered all sorts of things about Anne Meredith. Things that pointed to her not only being an habitual criminal, but also a murderer as well.

(RHODA looks across at MRS. OLIVER, who averts her gaze.)

That's right, isn't it, Mrs. Oliver?

MRS. OLIVER. I was only doing my duty – as a citizen.

BATTLE. Yes. However, I've gone ahead. *(He takes the score-cards from his pocket.)* It started with the bridge score-cards and Mrs. Oliver's assessment of each of the four players character. *(He turns to DESPARD.)* Let's take you, Major. A man with any amount of nerve. Accustomed to making quick decisions. You're not just at home when facing danger – you're actually enjoying it. And, when we look at how you placed your cards on the table these characteristics come into play as well. *(holding up the major's score-card)* Also that you're a man who likes to know exactly where he's going. Yes, you could have killed Shaitana. But, you would have faced up to him. Confronted him. *(He looks at another score-card.)* Mrs. Lorrimer, of course, was a brilliant bridge player... Cool. Calculated. Quick. Clean. Decisive. But, only because she *planned* every move she was going to make well in advance. *(then)* I would have accepted her confession readily – indeed, I was prepared to – because she had the intelligence to plan the perfect murder. But, she *insisted* that she killed Shaitana on the spur of the moment. *(He waves the score-card.)* Her card showed her to be the opposite of the kind of person who would kill in this way. But, I have to admit that her suicide almost fooled me. for a brief moment, I believed that I had misjudged her and that she had murdered him after all. But, then Anne Meredith was playing a very strange hand...

RHODA. I can hardly believe it. We were friends.

BATTLE. *(producing another score-card)* She was no friend of yours, Miss Dawes. Her score-card showed her to be a timid – reticent – bridge player. *Unwilling* to take risks. But... if she was afraid. Well, put it this way: when a dog corners a cat, the cat cowers – shaking with fear – but, if there's a way out – it will defend itself – suddenly *pounce* – and quite often win... *(then)* Her card also showed her to be a very economical young lady. *(He turns the card over.)* She actually turned it over and used the back. A sign of poverty? Or at least someone not used to having a great deal of money to spare. And, yet, she dressed so well. *(He turns to **MRS. OLIVER.**)* And, also – if we are to believe Mrs. Oliver – she set a little trap for Miss Meredith. Didn't you?

RHODA. The stockings!

BATTLE. That's right, isn't it, Mrs. Oliver?

*(**MRS. OLIVER** doesn't reply. She just looks more and more uneasy.)*

Well. *Apparently* – there were two pairs missing...

RHODA. How awful. We were supposed to be helping.

BATTLE. Anne Meredith was. *According* to *Mrs. Oliver* – she was helping herself. *(then)* Now we come to the card she was hiding up her sleeve. I'm referring to Combeacre and Mrs. Benson, whose death was thought to be an accident. Well, she was there only three weeks, so what *possible* motive could she have for murdering Mrs. Benson? I draw your attention to my analogy of the cornered cat. What would frighten her so much that she be forced to – strike! I believe Mrs. Benson caught her stealing and threatened her with the police. It was enough to tip the balance. That's why she tried to murder you. Because you might have told someone.

RHODA. But, I did tell someone...

(**RHODA** *turns to* **MRS. OLIVER** *who averts her eyes.*)

BATTLE. And, Mrs. Oliver made certain I knew.

(*He stops. The others wait for a moment, nothing else is forthcoming.*)

ROBERTS. Well. Er – thank you for putting us in the picture. If that's all, I'll be on my way. I've got rather a large evening surgery to attend to.

(*He gets up.*)

BATTLE. Oh, give me a few more minutes, please, Doctor. I haven't played my trump card yet. (*to* **MRS. OLIVER**) Have I, Mrs. Oliver?

MRS. OLIVER. (*through clenched teeth*) I don't know.

BATTLE. Oh, you do. You actually dealt it. (*He turns back to* **ROBERTS.**) Sit down, Doctor. As a bridge player you'll really appreciate it, it's a grand slam.

ROBERTS. Well, I can't stay too long. Excuse me. (*He sits on the arm of the sofa.*)

(**BATTLE** *takes a deep breath, then brings out another score-card with a flourish.*)

BATTLE. In the third rubber, we find the figure of fifteen hundred above the line and five hundred and sixty below the line. That could only mean one thing: a grand slam. Vulnerable. Doubled. And *redoubled.* If a murder was to be committed – in the very extraordinary circumstances that prevailed the night Shaitana died – when a game of bridge was in progress, then there were two very serious risks to be taken into consideration. One: the victim might very well call out. Two: the others might see it happen. As to the first risk nothing could be done about it. It was a case of gambler's luck. The second risk could be taken care of by making sure that, no matter what, the players attentions were wholly on the game and would not be distracted by anything else. A grand slam, vulnerable, doubled, and redoubled is – *riveting. (He slowly turns to face* **MRS. OLIVER.**) I can't prove you murdered Shaitana – *(Then a quick spin on his heels and he's face to face with* **ROBERTS.**) – Dr. Roberts.

(**ROBERTS** *is so taken aback his mouth drops open.*)

I can't even prove you infected Mr. Craddock's shaving brush. But, you did. And how you managed to murder Mrs. Craddock will probably remain a mystery forever. The one thing I can prove is that *you* murdered Mrs. Lorrimer.

(stunned silence)

ROBERTS. *(moving away downstage)* That's absurd!

BATTLE. *(as fast as he can go)* You bluffed your way into her bedroom when she was still asleep under the influence of Veronal. Like the card player you are – you bluff again. Pretend to see at a glance that she's dying. Pack the maid off for brandy and hot water. You're alone in the room with the *sleeping* Mrs. Lorrimer. You can freely *murder* again. Except – you were not alone!

ROBERTS. I... *(He is about to say "was alone," but he stops himself)* Oh, no.

You're not catching me out that way, Superintendent. I'm aware of the stupid little tricks you policemen play.

(They stand facing each other: two combatants on the field of **BATTLE.**)

(**BATTLE** *turns, crosses to the door and opens it.*)

BATTLE. Would you come in please, Mr. Stephens?

(**STEPHENS** *enters wearing a cloth cap and overalls. He has big whiskers and sideburns.*)

Mr. Stephens, is there anyone in this room you recognize?

STEPHENS. *(pointing at* **ROBERTS***)* Yes, him.

BATTLE. When did you last see him and under what circumstances?

STEPHENS. It was here wannit? I was cleaning the windows. About eight this morning. The lady of the house was in bed asleep. *(he points)* Then he comes in with the maid, who dashes straight back out again. The lady starts to wake up. He pulls up her sleeve – and gives her an injection. And she went out like a light again.

ROBERTS. *(flustered)* Well, of course I did. I was giving her a restorative…

BATTLE. Pentothal. Injected intravenously – in large doses – and in conjunction with Veronal – deadly! *(after a moment)* And that, Dr. Roberts, I *can* prove.

(**ROBERTS** *looks frantically for an escape route.*)

You've been dealt a very poor hand this time, Doctor. You may as well put your cards on the table.

ROBERTS. Well, it seems I can't bluff my way out of this one then, Superintendent.

BATTLE. I'm afraid not.

ROBERTS. Well, I'm not sorry I did it. I did kill Shaitana. He was a devil. He tormented all of us. To me it was not murder. It was retribution. *(then)* Very well. I'm ready.

BATTLE. Sergeant! Take Dr. Roberts down to the station. I'll be along to charge him later.

O'CONNOR. *(to* **ROBERTS***)* This way.

(*With great dignity* **ROBERTS** *exits, followed by* **O'CONNOR**.)

BATTLE. *(turning to* **MRS. ROBERTS***)* Thank you, Mrs. Oliver. I'm sorry to have put you through it with our little charade just now.

MRS. OLIVER. I was beginning to believe that *I* was guilty.

BATTLE. *(turning to* **RHODA** *and* **DESPARD***)* Well, that's the end of it. May I wish you both great happiness.

MRS. OLIVER. That goes for me too.

RHODA. Thank you.

DESPARD. Thank you.

RHODA. Wasn't it lucky the window cleaner was there this morning?

BATTLE. *Lucky?* There was no luck attached to it. *That* was my ace of trumps. *(to* **STEPHENS***)* All right, Constable Stephens. You can get back into uniform now.

STEPHENS. Thank you, sir. Er – did you say something about a day off if it worked out...

BATTLE. Did I? I don't remember a word about it.

STEPHENS. Yes, sir. Thank you, sir.

*(***STEPHENS** *exits.)*

RHODA. There was no window cleaner...

DESPARD. So no-one saw Dr. Roberts murder Mrs. Lorrimer.

BATTLE. *I* saw him. *(He taps his head.)* In here.

DESPARD. Well done, sir.

*(***BATTLE** *beams triumphantly.)*

MRS. OLIVER. *(standing up)* Just one moment, if you please, Superintendent. You can't take all the credit for solving this case. May I remind you, I said Dr. Roberts was the murderer right at the start.

(They all turn to look at her.)

Well, I did... Didn't I?

(curtain)

FURNITURE AND PROPERTY LIST

ACT ONE

Scene I: **SHAITANA**'s drawing-room.

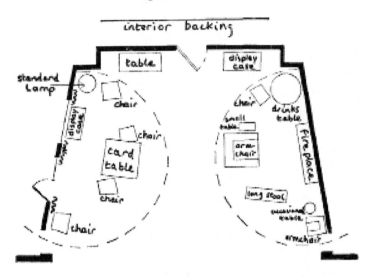

Onstage: Display cabinet right. *In it:* snuff boxes
Standard lamp
5 upright chairs
Card table with baize top. *On it:* three glasses of sherry
  (for **ANNE, DESPARD, ROBERTS**)
Downstage french window open
Table upstage right. *On it:* ornaments
Display case upstage left. *Inside:* snuff boxes. *On top:* glass
  of sherry (for **MRS. LORRIMER**)
Drinks table. *On it:* table lamp, telephone, bottles of
  drink, tray containing bottle of sherry and glasses
In fireplace: poker
On mantelpiece: 2 lamps, ornaments
Large winged armchair
Small table. *On it:* stiletto, ashtray
Plain armchair downstage left
Occasional table downstage left
Long low stool

Scene II: **SHAITANA**'s drawing-room
Set: On card table: playing cards, 4 complete bridge score-
                  cards, pencils, ashtray, glasses
Offstage: Tray. *On it:* coffee pot, sugar bowl, milk jug, 6 cups and
                  saucers (**MARY**)
Personal: **MRS. OLIVER:** large handbag containing Cox's apple

Scene III: **SHAITANA**'s drawing-room
Set: On small table: notepad and pencil (for **BATTLE**)
Personal: **MRS. OLIVER:** large handbag
                MRS. LORRIMER: evening bag
                ANNE: evening bag

Scene IV: **DR. ROBERT**'s surgery left

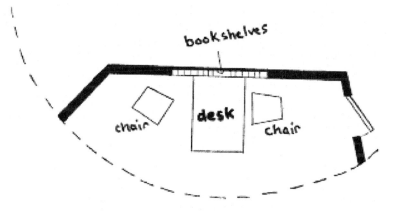

Onstage: Desk. *On it:* lamp, telephone, folders
                2 upright chairs
                Books on shelves
                Picture on wall left set askew
                Picture on wall right
Personal: **MISS BURGESS:** glasses on chain

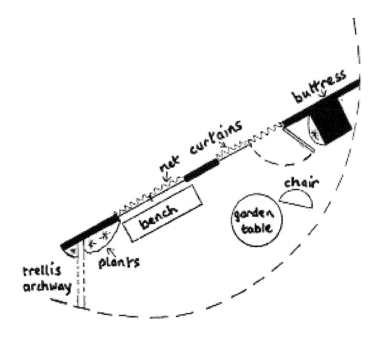

Onstage:	Bench
	Garden table. *On it:* ashtray
	Garden chair
	Upstage french window open
Offstage:	Unopened letter (**RHODA**)
Personal:	**MRS. OLIVER:** large handbag. *In it:* large Cox's apple
	DESPARD: piece of paper in pocket
	BATTLE: notepad and pencil in pocket
	SHAITANA's drawing-room
Strike:	From drinks table: tray of coffee
	From table downstage left: coffee cup
	From card table: all items
Set:	On card table: notepad (for **O'CONNOR**)
Re-set	Large winged armchair and small table as before

ACT TWO

Scene I: **MRS. LORRIMER**'s drawing-room

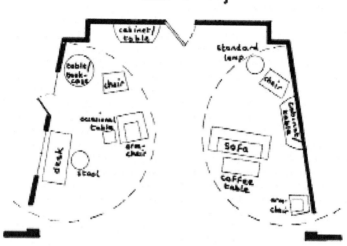

Onstage:	Desk. *On it:* paper, envelopes, pen, 1 letter written, 1 envelope with stamp
	Stool
	Armchair right. *On it:* cushion
	Occasional table
	Upstage french window open
	Round table with shelves containing books
	2 winged chairs. *On them:* cushions
	Cabinet. *On it:* ornaments, vase of flowers
	Standard lamp
	Sofa
	Coffee table. *On it:* tray containing tea set for two
	Cabinet. *On it:* 2 decanters, vase of flowers. *On shelves:* ornaments
	Small armchair downstage left
Personal:	**ANNE**: handbag

MRS. OLIVER's flat left

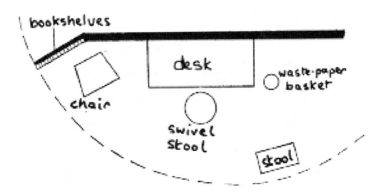

Onstage:	Upright chair. *On floor around it:* scattered books
	Desk. *On it:* typewriter containing page of type, wire
	tray containing folders and papers, telephone,
	books, brown paper bag of Cox's apples (for
	MRS OLIVER). *Propped against* right *leg:* cardboard
	box containing eighteen packets of stockings and
	one pair loose
	Waste-paper basket
	Swivel stool
	Stool left. *On it:* pile of books
	Books scattered on floor upstage left
	Shelves containing books
Personal:	**RHODA:** handbag, wrist-watch
	ANNE: handbag
	MRS. OLIVER: Cox's apple in pocket
	MRS. LORRIMER's drawing-room
Onstage:	As before
	MRS. OLIVER's flat left
Set:	On desk: half-chewed apple (for **BATTLE**)
Personal:	**MRS. OLIVER:** Cox's apple
	MRS. LORRIMER's drawing-room
Strike:	From coffee table: tea tray
Set:	On occasional table: glass of whisky

Scene II: The same

Strike:	From occasional table: glass of whisky
Personal:	**ROBERTS:** opened letter and small bottle of pills

in pocket
DORIS: handkerchief

WENDON LODGE right

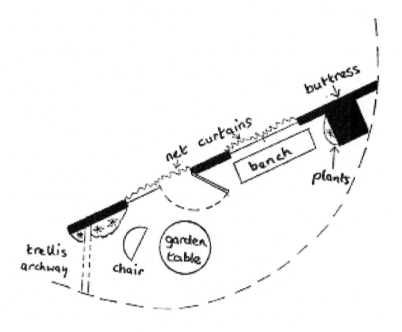

Re-set:	Bench
	Garden table
	Garden chair
Check:	Downstage french window open
Offstage:	Notepad, pen and purse (**RHODA**)
Personal:	**MAJOR DESPARD:** cigarettes, matches

Scene III: **MRS. LORRIMER**'s drawing-room

Onstage:	As before
Personal:	**MRS. OLIVER:** large handbag
	RHODA: handbag
	BATTLE: 4 completed bridge score-cards in pocket

LIGHTING PLOT

Practical fittings required: wall brackets, table lamps, standard lamp
One exterior and various interior settings

ACT ONE, Scene I Early evening in summer
To open: Late sunshine effect through windows
Cue 1   As guests exit to dinner
             Blackout

ACT ONE, Scene II Evening
To open: All practicals on
Cue 2   **ANNE** screams
             Blackout

ACT ONE, Scene III Evening
To open: All practicals on
Cue 3   **BATTLE:** "I'm sure you don't."
             Blackout

ACT ONE, Scene IV
To open: General interior lighting on **ROBERTS'** surgery left
Cue 4   **ROBERTS** starts laughing
             *Cross-fade to Wendon Lodge right: exterior
             sunshine effect*
Cue 5   **RHODA:** "Why did you lie to
             Superintendent Battle?"
             Fade to blackout
Cue 6   When ready
             *Bring up lighting in drawing-room to give bright
             sunshine effect through windows*

ACT TWO, Scene I Afternoon
To open: Sunshine effect through windows
Cue 7   **ANNE** turns away
             Fade to blackout
Cue 8   When ready
             *Bring up interior lighting on **MRS. OLIVER**'s
             flat left*
Cue 9   **MRS. OLIVER:** "Seventeen..."
             Fade to blackout
Cue 10   When ready
             Bring up general daylight effect on drawing-room
Cue 11   **ROBERTS:** "And I think you do too."
             Fade to blackout

Cue 12	When ready
	Bring up interior lighting on **MRS. OLIVER**'s *flat left*
Cue 13	**BATTLE:** "… she knows who murdered Shaitana.")
	Fade to blackout
Cue 14	When ready
	Bring up early evening sunlight effect on drawing-room
Cue 15	**BATTLE:** " – didn't you?"
	Blackout

ACT TWO, Scene II Morning

To open:	Bright sunshine effect in drawing-room
Cue 16	**BATTLE** and **O'CONNOR** rush out
	Blackout
Cue 17	When ready
	Bring up exterior sunshine effect on Wendon Lodge right
Cue 18	**BATTLE:** "… a few more shocks to come."
	Blackout

ACT TWO, Scene III Afternoon

| *To open:* | Sunshine effect in drawing-room |
| *No cues* | |

EFFECTS PLOT

ACT I

ACT II

CPSIA information can be obtained
at www.ICGtesting.com
Printed in the USA
LVOW13s0621140717
541333LV00036B/1173/P